HOOKED ON INDEPENDENT STUDY!

A Programmed Approach to Library Skills for Grades 3 Through 8

Marguerite Lewis

Illustrated by Pamela J. Kudla

THE CENTER FOR APPLIED
RESEARCH IN EDUCATION
West Nyack, New York 10995

ISBN 0-87628-405-5

THE CENTER FOR APPLIED
RESEARCH IN EDUCATION
West Nyack, New York 10995

Printed in the United States of America

Dedicated to our sons, Paul and Mark, who have shown me through their own experiences, that hard work, perseverance, and the ability to recognize one's own strengths and weaknesses, will eventually bring success.

About the Author
and the Illustrator

MARGUERITE LEWIS was a Library Media Specialist in the Bethlehem Central School District, Delmar, New York for 20 years. She received her Bachelor of Science degree from Boston University and her Master's Degree in Educational Communications from the State University of New York at Albany.

Mrs. Lewis has published articles, activities, and puzzles in professional and children's magazines. She is also the creator of *Library Bingo* and the co-creator with Pamela J. Lewis Kudla of *Library Curriculum Flashcards,* both published by Larlin Corporation, Marietta, Georgia. Mrs. Lewis also teamed with Pamela Kudla to write *Hooked on Research! Ready-to-Use Projects and Crosswords for Practice in Basic Library Skills* (1984), *Hooked on Reading! 114 Wordsearch and Crossword Puzzles Based on the Newbery and Caldecott Award Winners* (1986), and *Hooked on Library Skills! A Sequential Activities Program for Grades K–6* (1988), all published by The Center for Applied Research in Education. Mrs. Lewis is currently working on freelance projects.

PAMELA J. KUDLA received her Bachelor's Degree in Graphic Design from Rochester Institute of Technology, Rochester, New York. She was Design Consultant for *New York Alive* magazine, as well as Assistant Art Director for Communication and Design, an advertising agency in Latham, New York, and an Art Director for B. Sterling Benkhart, Ltd., an advertising and photography studio in Newport, Rhode Island. Mrs. Kudla is currently working on freelance projects.

About *Hooked on Independent Study!*

The purpose of this resource for teachers and librarians is to provide a systematic, programmed approach to library and information retrieval skills that involves students in assuming responsibility for their own learning. With this approach, the student reads, reviews, reinforces, and practices the necessary information retrieval skill. When reviewing and practicing, the student covers the answers with a marker, then removes the marker and self-corrects the work. When the student feels the information has been mastered, he/she assumes the responsibility of taking a test. Mastery of the skill is demonstrated when the student successfully completes the test.

For easy, effective use, *Hooked on Independent Study* is organized into 12 basic units corresponding to 12 major topics covered in the library skills curriculum at the upper elementary and middle school levels. Each unit presents a sequence of reproducible materials for learning a particular set of skills and can be copied just as it is, as many times as needed, for individual or group use. The units may be completed in any order desired and include:

1. Parts of a Book
2. Concepts of the Story
3. Card Catalog
4. Encyclopedia
5. Dewey Decimal Classification System
6. Almanac
7. Atlas
8. *The Readers' Guide to Periodical Literature*
9. Famous First Facts
10. *Bartlett's Familiar Quotations*
11. *Roget's International Thesaurus*
12. *Guinness Book of World Records*

Each unit contains one or more learning segments consisting of information and activity pages followed by a review and test frame. Answer keys for the test frames in each unit are given at the end, along with reproducible pattern markers for students' use as they complete the unit activities.

This programmed approach to library skills is appropriate for all students in grades 3 through 8 and can be administered by either the teacher or the library media specialist. It is designed to:

—lead the student through a progression of skills; presenting, reviewing, and reinforcing information retrieval. The skills are grouped in small steps to allow the student to practice mostly correct responses.

—lead the student independently from the known to the unknown, continuously building on the information previously introduced.

—provide the student with immediate confirmation of correct or incorrect answers.

—allow the student to progress at his/her own speed.

Short segments of information are presented. The student learns the information, covers the answers with a marker, then reviews and reinforces the information through writing answers to questions or completing activities. The student then self-corrects the answers. If the student "cheats" by not covering the answers, the act of reading the questions and writing the answers still provides one form of review and reinforcement. In any case, since there is a test frame at the end of each unit learning segment, the student quickly realizes that the test frame cannot be successfully completed if he/she has not mastered the skill.

If the student encounters difficulty in any area, the teacher/librarian can coach or drill the student through the use of different or additional activities. Students are thus able to progress at their own rate of speed without having to wait for others to catch up or feeling stressed due to preferring to work at a slower pace. The student moves through each unit independently. Where understanding of the skill comes easily, he/she needs no coaching or drill. The teacher/librarian coaches and drills the student individually only in the areas where extra assistance is needed.

You will find *Hooked on Independent Study* is a versatile instructional tool that may be used:

- To introduce and teach a skill independently to a full class.
- As additional instruction for students who need review and reinforcement.
- As primary instruction for a student who enters the school after the skill has been taught.
- As primary instruction for individual gifted and talented students.
- As a means to motivate students through use of an alternate method of instruction.

Through *Hooked on Independent Study* students begin to take responsibility for their own learning of library and information retrieval skills. Each unit provides information, review reinforcement, practice, and testing. Students can move through the material in each unit at their own rate, receiving coaching and drilling from you, the teacher or librarian, where needed.

Marguerite Lewis

Table of Contents

UNIT 1

Parts of a Book

Name _____

Date _____

UNIT 1: PARTS OF A BOOK
CHECK-OFF SHEET

DIRECTIONS: Below you will find the names of each activity sheet in UNIT 1. Check off each sheet as it is completed.

THE PHYSICAL PARTS 1–1	
THE PHYSICAL PARTS—REVIEW PAGE 1–2	
THE CONCEPTS 1–3	
THE CONCEPTS—ACTIVITY PAGE 1–4	
THE CONCEPTS—REVIEW PAGE 1–5	
TEST FRAME 1–6	
TITLE PAGE 1–7	
TITLE PAGE—ACTIVITY PAGE 1–8	
TITLE PAGE—TEST FRAME 1–9	
TABLE OF CONTENTS 1–10	
TABLE OF CONTENTS—ACTIVITY PAGE - A 1–11	
TABLE OF CONTENTS—ACTIVITY PAGE - B 1–12	
TABLE OF CONTENTS—ACTIVITY PAGE - C 1–13	
PREFACE, FOREWORD, OR INTRODUCTION 1–14	
PREFACE, FOREWORD, OR INTRODUCTION—ACTIVITY PAGE 1–15	
DEDICATION PAGE 1–16	
DEDICATION PAGE—ACTIVITY PAGE 1–17	
REVIEW PAGE 1–18	
TEST FRAME 1–19	
APPENDIX 1–20	
GLOSSARY 1–21	
GLOSSARY—ACTIVITY PAGE 1–22	
INDEX 1-23	
INDEX—USING THE INDEX 1–24	
INDEX—ACTIVITY PAGE 1–25	
REVIEW PAGE 1–26	
TEST FRAME 1–27	

Name _____

Date _____

PARTS OF A BOOK: THE PHYSICAL PARTS OF A BOOK

A. A book is made up of parts. The major parts are:

1. SPINE. The SPINE, also called the backbone of the book, holds the cover and pages together.

2. COVER. The COVER, made of heavy material, protects the pages. There is a front cover and a back cover.

3. PAGES. The PAGES, also called the leaves, are the papers on which the text or the words are printed.

4. TEXT. The TEXT is the words that are printed on the pages.

5. ILLUSTRATIONS. The ILLUSTRATIONS are the pictures found on all or some of the pages.

6. DUST JACKET. The DUST JACKET, also called the book jacket, is a colorful paper cover that helps to protect the cover of the book.

DIRECTIONS: Select a book or use the one assigned to you. Follow the directions.

1. Put your hand on the SPINE. Run your thumb and forefinger up and down the SPINE.

2. Put your hand on the front COVER. Put your hand on the back COVER.

3. Open the book. Select one PAGE. Read one paragraph. Close the book.

4. Open the book. Select one page. Put your hand on the TEXT. Close the book.

5. Open the book. Locate and put your hand on one ILLUSTRATION. Close the book.

6. Put your hand on the DUST JACKET.

When you feel you have mastered this information, go on to sheet 1–2.

© 1990 by The Center for Applied Research in Education

Name _____

Date _____

PARTS OF A BOOK: THE PHYSICAL PARTS OF THE BOOK—REVIEW PAGE

DIRECTIONS: Cover the answers with your marker. Answer the following questions. Uncover the answers and check your work. Correct if necessary.

1. The backbone of the book is called the

   _____.   spine

2. The spine holds the _____   cover

   and the _____   pages

   together.

3. The pages are the paper on which the

   text or the _____   words

   are printed.

4. The pictures in the book are called the

   _____.   illustrations

5. The _____   dust jacket

   or book jacket protects the cover and pages.

When you feel you have mastered this information, go on to sheet 1–3.

Name _____

Date _____

PARTS OF A BOOK: THE CONCEPTS

A. The concepts of the book are:

1. AUTHOR. An AUTHOR is a person who writes a book.

2. TITLE. The TITLE is the name of the book.

3. ILLUSTRATOR. An ILLUSTRATOR is a person who supplies the pictures for a book.

4. PUBLISHER. A PUBLISHER is a person or company that produces the book in printed form.

5. PLACE OF PUBLICATION. The PLACE OF PUBLICATION is the city in which the PUBLISHER is located.

6. COPYRIGHT. The COPYRIGHT is the permission to copy and sell the book.

7. COPYRIGHT DATE. The COPYRIGHT DATE is the date the book is printed and sold.

DIRECTIONS: Select a book or use the one assigned to you. Follow the directions.

B. Find and write the following concepts:

1. AUTHOR _____

2. TITLE _____

3. ILLUSTRATOR _____

4. PUBLISHER _____

5. PLACE OF PUBLICATION _____

6. COPYRIGHT DATE _____

When you feel you have mastered this information, go on to sheet 1–4.

Name _____

Date _____

Parts of a Book

PARTS OF A BOOK: THE CONCEPTS: ACTIVITY PAGE

DIRECTIONS: Using the information on the book pictured below, complete the following activity.

The Little Chipmunk

by Alex Brown

Illustrations by

Jane Brown

The Jones Press
New York
1989

Author _____

Title _____

Illustrator _____

Publisher _____

Place of
Publication _____ Copyright Date _____

Turn in this sheet to be checked. When you have successfully completed this page, go on to sheet 1–5.

PARTS OF A BOOK: CONCEPTS: REVIEW PAGE

DIRECTIONS: Cover the answers with your marker. Answer the following questions. Uncover the answers and check your work. Correct if necessary.

1.   A person who writes a book is an

_____.   author

2.   The name of the book is the

_____.   title

3.   The person who supplies the pictures for the book is the

_____.   illustrator

4.   The _____ is responsible   publisher

for producing the book in printed form.

5.   The city in which the publisher is located is the

                                                                                 place of
_____.   publication

6.   Permission to copy and sell the book is the

_____.   copyright

7.   The date the book is printed is the

                                                                                 copyright
_____.   date

When you feel you have mastered the parts of the book and the concepts of the book, found on the last four pages, go on to sheet 1–6.

Name _____

Date _____

PARTS OF A BOOK: TEST FRAME

DIRECTIONS: Answer the following questions. As this is a test frame, no answers are given.

1. The backbone of the book is called the _____.

2. The heavy material that protects the pages is called the

    _____.

3. The _____ is the words that are printed on the page.

4. The pictures are called the _____.

5. The _____ protects the covers and adds to the attractiveness of the book.

6. The person who writes a book is called an _____.

7. The name of the book is called the _____.

8. The _____ supplies the pictures for the book.

9. The _____ is responsible for producing the book.

10. The _____ tells where the publisher is located.

11. The permission to copy from a book is called the _____.

12. The date the book is published is called the _____.

Turn in this test to be corrected. When you pass the test, go on to sheet 1–7.

Name _____

Date _____

PARTS OF A BOOK: TITLE PAGE

A. The TITLE PAGE can also be called the business page of the book.

1. On the TITLE PAGE, you will find:

   a. The TITLE of the book.

   b. The AUTHOR of the book.

   c. The ILLUSTRATOR if the book has pictures.

   d. The PUBLISHER of the book.

   e. The PLACE OF PUBLICATION, where the publisher is located.

   f. The COPYRIGHT DATE which may be found at the bottom of the TITLE PAGE or on the back of the TITLE PAGE or both.

DIRECTIONS: Select a book or use the one assigned to you.

1. Locate the TITLE PAGE.

   a. Put your fingers on the TITLE. Read it to yourself.

   b. Put your fingers on the AUTHOR'S name. Read it to yourself.

   c. Put your fingers on the ILLUSTRATOR'S name. Read it to yourself.

   d. Put your fingers on the PUBLISHER'S name. Read it to yourself.

   e. Put your fingers on the PLACE OF PUBLICATION. Read it to yourself.

   f. Locate the COPYRIGHT DATE. Look for the symbol ©. Put your fingers on the date. Read it to yourself.

When you feel you have mastered this information, go on to sheet 1–8.

Name _____

Date _____

PARTS OF A BOOK: THE TITLE PAGE: ACTIVITY PAGE

DIRECTIONS: Locate a book or use the one assigned to you. Using the title page, fill in the following information.

1. Title _____

2. Author _____

3. Illustrator _____

4. Publisher _____

5. Place of Publication _____

6. Copyright Date _____

DIRECTIONS: Locate another book or use another book assigned to you. Using the title page, fill in the following information.

1. Title _____

2. Author _____

3. Illustrator _____

4. Publisher _____

5. Place of Publication _____

6. Copyright Date _____

Turn in the books and this sheet to be corrected. When you have successfully completed this sheet, go on to sheet 1–9.

Name _____

Date _____

PARTS OF A BOOK: THE TITLE PAGE: TEST FRAME

DIRECTIONS: Answer the following questions. As this is a test frame, no answers are given.

1.   The business page of the book is called the _____.

2.   The following information is found on this page.

     a. _____

     b. _____

     c. _____

     d. _____

     e. _____

3.   The following information is found on the title page or on the back of this page.

     a. _____

4.   Define the answers you wrote for question 2.

     a. _____.

     b. _____.

     c. _____.

     d. _____.

     e. _____.

5.   Define the answer you wrote for question 3.

     a. _____.

Turn in this test to be corrected. When you pass the test, go on to sheet 1–10.

Name _____

Date _____

PARTS OF A BOOK: TABLE OF CONTENTS

Fiction and nonfiction books are divided into sections called CHAPTERS.

The CHAPTERS are listed in the front of the book. This listing is called the CONTENTS or TABLE OF CONTENTS.

The CONTENTS or TABLE OF CONTENTS lists the number of chapters and the page on which each begins.

Sometimes the CHAPTERS have titles. Sometimes the CHAPTERS do not have titles.

Table of Contents

Chapter 1 4   Chapter 5 53

Chapter 2 11   Chapter 6 72

Chapter 3 25

Chapter 4 40

DIRECTIONS: Cover the answers with your marker. Answer the following questions. Uncover the answers and check your work. Correct if necessary.

1. Fiction and nonfiction books are divided into sections called

    _____.   chapters

2. This listing is called the _____   contents

    or _____.   table of contents

3. The table of contents lists the number of _____   chapters

    and the _____ on which each begins.   page

4. The table of contents is found in the _____   front

    of the book.

5. Sometimes the chapters have _____.   titles

    Sometimes the chapters do not have _____.   titles

When you feel you have mastered this information, go on to sheet 1–11.

Name _____

Date _____

PARTS OF A BOOK: THE TABLE OF CONTENTS:
ACTIVITY PAGE—A

> *DIRECTIONS:* Below is a copy of a table of contents. Cover the answers with your marker. Answer the questions below the table of contents. Uncover the answers and check your work. Correct if necessary.

CONTENTS	
Chapter 1	4
Chapter 2	9
Chapter 3	16
Chapter 4	21
Chapter 5	24
Chapter 6	29

1. How many chapters does this book contain?

    _____   6

2. On what page does Chapter 4 begin?

    _____   21

3. How many pages are included in Chapter 1?

    _____   5

4. How many pages are included in Chapter 5?

    _____   5

Turn in this sheet to be checked. When you have successfully completed this sheet, go on to sheet 1–12.

Parts of a Book

PARTS OF A BOOK: THE TABLE OF CONTENTS: ACTIVITY PAGE—B

DIRECTIONS: Below is a copy of a table of contents. Cover the answers with your marker. Answer the questions below the table of contents. Uncover the answers and check your work. Correct if necessary.

TABLE OF CONTENTS

1.	Africa	6
2.	Antarctica	13
3.	Asia	20
4.	Australia	28
5.	Europe	35
6.	North America	42
7.	South America	50

1. How many chapters does this book contain?

   _____   7

2. On what page does the chapter about Asia begin?

   _____   20

3. How many pages does the chapter on Europe contain?

   _____   7

4. If you were looking for information about Australia,

   you would turn to page _____.   28

Turn in this sheet to be checked. When you have successfully completed this sheet, go on to sheet 1–13.

Name _____

Date _____

**PARTS OF A BOOK: TABLE OF CONTENTS:
ACTIVITY PAGE—C**

DIRECTIONS: Select a fiction book or use the one assigned to you. Fill in the following information.

1. Author _____

2. Title _____

3. Illustrator _____

4. Publisher _____

5. Copyright Date _____

6. How many chapters are in this book? _____

7. Do the chapters have titles? Yes _____ No _____

DIRECTIONS: Select a nonfiction book or use the one assigned to you. Fill in the following information.

1. Author _____

2. Title _____

3. Illustrator _____

4. Publisher _____

5. Copyright Date _____

6. How many chapters are in the book? _____

7. Do the chapters have titles? Yes _____ No _____

Turn in this sheet and the books to be checked. When you have successfully completed this activity, go on to sheet 1–14.

Name _____

Date _____

PARTS OF A BOOK: PREFACE, FOREWORD, OR INTRODUCTION

Some books contain information or an explanation for the reader to read before reading the first chapter.

This information or explanation may be written by the author, the publisher, or another author.

There are three terms for this information or explanation. The three terms have the same meaning. The three terms are:

1. PREFACE
2. FOREWORD
3. INTRODUCTION

The PREFACE, FOREWORD, or INTRODUCTION is not part of the text, but is something the reader should know before reading the book.

The PREFACE, FOREWORD, or INTRODUCTION is located in the front of the book.

DIRECTIONS: Cover the answers with your marker. Answer the following questions. Uncover the answers and check your work. Correct if necessary.

1. Some books contain _____ or an   information

   _____ for the reader to read before reading   explanation

   the book.

2. This material is written by the _____,   author

   the _____ , or another   publisher

   _____.   author

3. This material is called the _____,   preface
                                                                      foreword
   _____, or _____.   introduction

When you feel you have mastered this information, go on to sheet 1–15.

Name _____

Date _____

PARTS OF A BOOK: PREFACE, FOREWORD, OR INTRODUCTION: ACTIVITY PAGE

DIRECTIONS: Locate a book containing a preface, foreword, or introduction or use the one assigned to you. Using the book, complete the following activities.

1. Author _____

2. Title _____

3. Illustrator _____

4. Publisher _____

5. Place of
   Publication _____ Copyright Date _____

6. Locate and read the PREFACE, FOREWORD, or INTRODUCTION.

   a. Which of the three terms is used for this information?

   _____

   b. Is the information written by the author, another author, or publisher?

   _____

   c. What is the purpose of this PREFACE, FOREWORD, or INTRODUCTION?

   _____

   _____

   _____

   _____

Turn in this sheet to be checked. When you have successfully completed this sheet, go on to sheet 1–16.

Name _____

Date _____

PARTS OF A BOOK: DEDICATION PAGE

An author and/or illustrator may wish to publicly thank a person or persons as a sign of affection or respect.

The author and/or illustrator write a short phrase in the front of the book, dedicating the book to the person or persons.

This is called the DEDICATION and is usually found on a separate page in the front of the book called the DEDICATION PAGE.

Not all books have a DEDICATION. The author and/or illustrator choose to have or to not have a DEDICATION.

DIRECTIONS: Cover the answers with your marker. Answer the following questions. Uncover the answers and check your work. Correct if necessary.

1. An author and/or illustrator may wish to publicly thank a

    person as a sign of _____   affection

    or _____ .   respect

2. This is called the _____ .   dedication

3. The page on which this is found is called the

    _____ .   dedication page

4. The author and/or illustrator choose to _____   have

    or _____ a dedication.   not have

5. The _____ page is located in the   dedication

    _____ of the book.   front

When you feel you have mastered this information, go on to sheet 1–17.

Name _____

Date _____

Parts
of a
Book

PARTS OF A BOOK: DEDICATION PAGE: ACTIVITY PAGE

DIRECTIONS: Locate the dedication in three books or use the ones assigned to you. Complete the following for each book.

1. Author _____

    Title _____

    Dedication _____

    _____

2. Author _____

    Title _____

    Dedication _____

    _____

3. Author _____

    Title _____

    Dedication _____

    _____

DIRECTIONS: Pretend you have written a book and wish to dedicate the book to someone. Write a dedication to that person on the lines below.

_____

_____

Turn in this sheet to be checked. When you have successfully completed this sheet, go on to sheet 1–18.

Name _____

Date _____

PARTS OF A BOOK: TABLE OF CONTENTS
PREFACE, FOREWORD, OR INTRODUCTION
DEDICATION PAGE: REVIEW PAGE

DIRECTIONS: Cover the answers with your marker. Answer the following questions. Uncover the answers and check your work. Correct if necessary.

1. Fiction and nonfiction books are divided into sections

   called _____.   chapters

2. The list of these chapters is called the

   _____.   table of contents

3. The list of chapters is found in the _____   front

   of the book.

4. An explanation or information for the reader before reading is

                                                               preface
   called the _____, _____,   foreword

   or _____.   introduction

5. This explanation or information may be written by the

                                                               author
   _____, _____,   publisher

   or another _____.   author

6. A thank you from the author and/or illustrator to a person or

   persons as a sign of affection or respect is called a

   _____.   dedication

7. All books have a dedication. (true) or (false)   false

When you feel you have mastered this information, go on to sheet 1–19.

Name _____

Date _____

PARTS OF A BOOK: TABLE OF CONTENTS
PREFACE, FOREWORD, OR INTRODUCTION
DEDICATION PAGE: TEST FRAME

DIRECTIONS: Answer the following questions. As this is a test frame, no answers are given.

1. Fiction and nonfiction books are divided into sections called _____.

2. The list of these chapters is called the _____

    or the _____.

3. The list of chapters is found in the _____ of the book.

4. The chapters may or may not have _____.

5. An explanation or information for the reader before reading the book is called the

    _____, _____,

    or _____.

6. This explanation or information may be written by the _____,

    the _____, or another _____.

7. This explanation or information is found in the _____ of the book.

8. A thank you from the author to a person or persons as a sign of affection or respect

    is called a _____.

9. The thank you is found in the _____ of the book.

Turn in this test to be corrected. When you have successfully completed this test, go on to sheet 1–20.

Name _____

Date _____

PARTS OF A BOOK: APPENDIX

Some nonfiction books contain an extra section at the back of the book just before the glossary.

This section gives extra information usually in the form of:

Copies of official documents   Diagrams   Maps

Charts   Letters   Tables

This section is called the APPENDIX.

DIRECTIONS: Cover the answers with your marker. Answer the following questions. Uncover the answers and check your work. Correct if necessary.

1. A section at the back of the book giving extra information is the

   _____.   appendix

2. This section gives information in the form of

   _____, _____,   copies of official documents, charts

   _____, _____,   diagrams, letters,

   _____, or _____.   maps, tables

DIRECTIONS: Locate a nonfiction book containing an appendix or use the one assigned to you. Fill in author and title. Locate the appendix.

1. Author   _____

2. Title   _____

3. What type of information is included in the appendix? _____

   _____

   _____

Turn in this sheet and book to be checked. When you have successfully completed this activity, go on to sheet 1–21.

Name _____

Date _____

PARTS OF A BOOK: GLOSSARY

Many nonfiction books contain words that may be unfamiliar to the reader.

These words may be listed alphabetically in the back of the book, giving the pronunciation and the definition of these words.

This listing is called a GLOSSARY.

Think of a GLOSSARY as a special dictionary prepared especially for the book.

Not all nonfiction books contain a GLOSSARY. The decision whether to have a GLOSSARY or not is up to the author and/or the publisher.

Glossary

antonym –
(án-tə-nim)
a word of
opposite meaning.
22

atlas ('at-ləs)
a bound collection
of maps . 27

book index
('buk 'in-,deks)
an alphabetical
list of the
main topics
covered in a book
17

DIRECTIONS: Cover the answers with your marker. Answer the following questions. Uncover the answers and check your work. Correct if necessary.

1. Many _____ books contain words that may be
   unfamiliar to the _____.

2. These words may be listed in the _____ of the book.

3. This listing is called a _____.

4. This listing gives the _____ and
   the _____ for each word.

5. This listing is a special _____
   prepared for the book.

nonfiction

reader

back

glossary

pronunciation

definition

dictionary

When you feel you have mastered this information, go on to sheet 1–22.

Name _____

Date _____

PARTS OF A BOOK: GLOSSARY: ACTIVITY PAGE

DIRECTIONS: Locate a nonfiction book containing a glossary or use the one assigned to you. Locate the glossary in the back of the book. Complete the following activities.

1. Choose a word beginning with the letter A. Write the word and the meaning.

   Word _____ Meaning _____

   _____

2. Choose a word beginning with the letter G. Write the word and the meaning.

   Word _____ Meaning _____

   _____

3. Choose a word beginning with the letter L. Write the word and the meaning.

   Word _____ Meaning _____

   _____

4. Choose a word beginning with the letter P. Write the word and the meaning.

   Word _____ Meaning _____

   _____

5. Choose a word beginning with the letter W. Write the word and the meaning.

   Word _____ Meaning _____

   _____

6. Can you find any similarity or pattern to the kinds of words that are included in the glossary? Are they special words?

   _____

Turn in this sheet with the book to be checked. When you have successfully completed this sheet, go on to sheet 1–23.

Name _____

Date _____

Parts
of a
Book

PARTS OF A BOOK: INDEX

Many nonfiction books contain an alphabetical listing of the subjects found in the book.

This listing includes the subject and the page or pages on which information is located.

This alphabetical listing is called the INDEX.

The INDEX is located in the back of the book.

Index

Aaron, Hank
p. 78-80

Abolitionist
movement
p. 95-100

Absolute Zero
P. 87

Abstract Art
p. 121-122

DIRECTIONS: Cover the answers with your marker. Answer the following questions. Uncover the answers and check your work. Correct if necessary.

1. Many nonfiction books contain an _____   alphabetical

    listing of the _____ found in the book.   subjects

2. This listing contains the subject and the _____   page

    or _____ on which information is located.   pages

3. This alphabetical listing is called the _____.   index

4. This listing is located in the _____ of the book.   back

When you feel you have mastered this information, go on to sheet 1–24.

Name _____

Date _____

Parts of a Book

PARTS OF A BOOK: INDEX: USING THE INDEX

There are two important symbols used in the INDEX.
These symbols are the comma and the dash.

Look at the following example.

| Birds | 15, 22, 33–37 |

The comma separates the pages of information.
The dash includes the pages between the numbers.

The comma tells you there is information on page 15 and
page 22. There is no information on the pages between 15 and 22.

The dash tells you there is information on the pages between 33 and 37.
There are five pages of information.

There is a total of seven pages of information on birds.
These pages are 15, 22, 33, 34, 35, 36, and 37.

DIRECTIONS: Cover the answers with your marker. Answer the following questions. Uncover the answers and check your work. Correct if necessary.

1. The two important symbols used in an index are the

    _____ and the _____.   comma
                                                        dash

2. The _____ separates the pages of information.   comma

3. The _____ includes the pages between the numbers.   dash

When you feel you have mastered this information, go on to sheet 1–25.

Name _____

Date _____

PARTS OF A BOOK: INDEX: ACTIVITY PAGE

© 1990 by The Center for Applied Research in Education

DIRECTIONS: Locate a nonfiction book containing an index or use the one assigned to you. Complete the following activities.

1. Author _____

   Title   _____

2. Choose a subject in the index beginning with the letter B.

   Subject _____

   Page or pages on which information will be found _____

   Total number of pages of information _____

3. Choose a subject in the index beginning with the letter G.

   Page or pages on which information will be found _____

   Total number of pages of information _____

4. Choose a subject in the index beginning with the letter P.

   Page or pages on which information will be found _____

   Total number of pages of information _____

5. Choose a subject beginning with the letter S.

   Page or pages on which information will be found _____

   Total number of pages of information _____

6. Choose a subject beginning with the letter W.

   Page or pages on which information will be found _____

   Total number of pages of information _____

Turn in this sheet with the book to be checked. When you have successfully completed this activity, go on to sheet 1–26.

Name _____

Date _____

PARTS OF A BOOK: REVIEW PAGE

DIRECTIONS: Cover the answers with your marker. Answer the following questions. Uncover the answers and check your work. Correct if necessary.

1. A thank you from the author to someone who helped with

   the book is called a _____.   dedication

2. The chapters of a book are listed in the

   _____.   table of contents

3. A section at the back of the book containing extra material

   is called the _____.   appendix

4. An alphabetical listing of subjects and pages found in the back

   of the book is called the _____.   index

5. A small dictionary of special words or terms found in the book

   is called a _____.   glossary

6. Information given by the author to the reader before the book is

   read is called the _____,   preface

   _____,   foreword

   or _____.   introduction

When you feel you have mastered this information, go on to sheet 1-27.

Name _____

Date _____

PARTS OF A BOOK: TEST FRAME

DIRECTIONS: Answer the following questions. As this is a test frame, no answers
are given.

1. A section at the back of the book containing additional material is called the

_____.

2. A small dictionary of special words or terms found in the book is called the

_____.

3. Information given to the reader before the book is read is called the

_____, _____,

or _____.

4. A thank you from the author to someone who helped with the book is called the

_____.

5. The chapters of a book are listed in the _____

_____.

6. An alphabetical listing of subjects and pages found in the back of the book is called

the _____.

7. Which of the above pages or sections are found in the front of the book.

_____

_____

8. Which of the above pages or sections are found in the back of the book.

_____

_____

Turn in this sheet to be checked. When you successfully pass the test, go on to another Unit.

© 1990 by The Center for Applied Research in Education

UNIT 2

Concepts of the Story

Name _____

Date _____

UNIT 2: CONCEPTS OF THE STORY
CHECK-OFF SHEET

DIRECTIONS: Below you will find the names of each activity sheet in UNIT 2. Check off each sheet as it is completed.

PARTS OF THE STORY 2–1	
PARTS OF THE STORY—ACTIVITY PAGE 2–2	
CHARACTERS 2–3	
CHARACTERS—ACTIVITY PAGE 2–4	
PLOT 2–5	
SETTING 2–6	
DESCRIPTION 2–7	
DIALOGUE 2–8	
I VIEW PAGE 2–9	
REVIEW PAGE 2 2–10	
TEST FRAME 2–11	
ACTION 2–12	
THEME 2–13	
STYLE 2–14	
GENRE 2–15	
REVIEW PAGE 2–16	
TEST FRAME 2–17	

Name _____

Date _____

CONCEPTS OF THE STORY: PARTS OF THE STORY

Every story contains three parts.

1. *BEGINNING:* The introduction. You meet the important characters, find out the problem, and are given hints of the direction of the story.

2. *MIDDLE:* The action. The characters are developed and the plot unfolds.

3. *END:* The conclusion. The problem is solved, the loose ends are tied up, and the story comes to a satisfying conclusion.

DIRECTIONS: Cover the answers with your marker. Answer the following questions. Uncover the answers and check your work. Correct if necessary.

1. The introduction of the important characters and the problem

   take place in the _____ of the story. beginning

2. The characters are developed and the plot unfolds in the

   _____ of the story. middle

3. The problem is solved and all loose ends are tied up at the

   _____ of the story. end

4. The longest part of the story will probably be the

   _____. middle

When you feel you have mastered this information, go on to sheet 2–2.

Name _____

Date _____

CONCEPTS OF THE STORY: PARTS OF THE STORY: ACTIVITY PAGE

DIRECTIONS: Select two books that you have recently read. Tell briefly what happens in the beginning, the middle, and the end.

1. Author _____

    Title _____

    Beginning _____

    _____

    Middle _____

    _____

    End _____

    _____

2. Author _____

    Title _____

    Beginning _____

    _____

    Middle _____

    _____

    End _____

    _____

Turn in this sheet with the books to be checked. When you have successfully completed this activity, go on to sheet 2–3.

© 1990 by The Center for Applied Research in Education

Name _____

Date _____

CONCEPTS OF THE STORY: CHARACTERS

Whoever is in a story is called a CHARACTER.
A character may be a person, an animal, a fish,
a ghost, an airplane, a boat, or a train.

The most important character is called the
MAIN CHARACTER. The MAIN
CHARACTER can be compared to the star in a
play or TV show.

Other characters who are important are called
SUPPORTING CHARACTERS.

DIRECTIONS: Cover the answers with your marker. Answer the following questions.
Uncover the answers and check your work. Correct if necessary.

1. Whoever is in a story is called a _____.   character

2. The most important character is called the

    _____.   main character

3. Other characters who are important are called the

    _____   _____.   supporting
                                                                      characters

4. The three parts of the story are

    _____   beginning

    _____   middle

    _____.   end

When you feel you have mastered this information, go on to sheet 2–4.

Name _____

Date _____

PARTS OF THE BOOK: CHARACTERS: ACTIVITY PAGE

DIRECTIONS: Select three books that you have recently read. Complete the following activities.

1. Author _____

   Title _____

   Publisher _____ Copyright Date _____

   Main character _____

   Supporting characters _____

2. Author _____

   Title _____

   Publisher _____ Copyright Date _____

   Main character _____

   Supporting characters _____

3. Author _____

   Title _____

   Publisher _____ Copyright Date _____

   Main character _____

   Supporting characters _____

Turn in this sheet with the books to be checked. When you have successfully completed this activity, go on to sheet 2–5.

Name _____

Date _____

CONCEPTS OF THE STORY: PLOT

What a story is all about or what happens in a story is called the PLOT.

The PLOT can be defined as the plan of events in a story.

DIRECTIONS: Cover the answer with your marker. Answer the question. Uncover
the answer and check your work. Correct if necessary.

1. The plan of events or what the story is all about is called the

_____.   plot

DIRECTIONS: Select two books you have recently read. Complete the following
activities for each book.

1. Author _____   Title _____

Publisher _____   Copyright Date _____

Plot _____

_____

_____

2. Author _____   Title _____

Publisher _____   Copyright Date _____

Plot _____

_____

_____

Turn in this sheet with the books to be checked. When you have successfully completed this
activity, go on to sheet 2–6.

Name _____

Date _____

CONCEPTS OF THE STORY: SETTING

Where and when the story takes place or is set is called the SETTING.

For example: The story takes place in New York State in the late 1800s.

The story takes place in present day New York State.

The story takes place on the planet Mars in the late twenty-first century.

DIRECTIONS: Cover the answer with your marker. Answer the following question. Uncover your answer and check your work. Correct if necessary.

1. Where and when the story takes place is called the

_____.   setting

DIRECTIONS: Select a book that you have recently read. Complete the following activities.

1. Author _____

Title _____

Publisher _____ Copyright Date _____

Setting: Place _____

Time _____

Turn in this sheet with the book to be checked. When you have successfully completed this activity, go on to sheet 2–7.

Name _____

Date _____

CONCEPTS OF THE STORY: DESCRIPTION

The author paints pictures with words.

The author tells about a character, a place, or a thing in such a way that you can form a picture in your mind.

This is called the DESCRIPTION.

DIRECTIONS: Cover the answer with your marker. Answer the following question. Uncover the answer and check your work. Correct if necessary.

1. How the author paints pictures with words is called the

    _____.   description

DIRECTIONS: Select a book that you have recently read. Complete the following activities.

Author _____

Title _____

Publisher _____ Copyright Date _____

Select a short description of a character in the book.

" _____

_____

_____

_____

_____. "

Turn in this sheet with the book to be checked. When you have successfully completed this activity, go on to sheet 2–8.

Name _____

Date _____

CONCEPTS OF THE STORY: DIALOGUE

In a story or book, the actual words spoken by a character are enclosed in quotation marks.

The words contained between the quotation marks are called the DIALOGUE.

"Let's read this new story," said Jeff.

DIRECTIONS: Cover the answers with your marker. Answer the following questions. Uncover the answers and check your work. Correct if necessary.

1. In a story or book, the words spoken by a character are

    enclosed in _____.

    quotation marks

2. The words contained between these marks are called the

    _____.

    dialogue

DIRECTIONS: Select a book you have recently read. Complete the following activity.

Author _____

Title _____

Publisher _____ Copyright Date _____

Give an example of dialogue from the book. Remember to write who is talking.

_____

_____ Page _____

Turn in this sheet to be checked. When you have successfully completed this activity, go on to sheet 2–9.

Name _____

Date _____

CONCEPTS OF THE STORY: REVIEW PAGE

CHARACTERS   **DESCRIPTION**
DIALOGUE   **PLOT**
SETTING

DIRECTIONS: Cover the answers with your marker. Answer the following questions. Uncover the answers and check your work. Correct if necessary.

1. The plan of events or what the story is all about is called the

   _____.

            plot

2. Where the story takes place is called a

   _____.

            setting

3. Whoever is in a story is called a

   _____.

            character

4. How the author tells about a character, a place, or a thing is called

   the _____.

            description

5. The actual words of a character enclosed in quotation marks are

   called the _____.

            dialogue

When you feel you have mastered this information, go on to sheet 2–10.

Name _____

Date _____

CONCEPTS OF THE STORY: REVIEW PAGE 2

CHARACTERS   DESCRIPTION
DIALOGUE   PLOT
SETTING

DIRECTIONS: Select a book that you have recently read. Do not use one that you have already used. Complete the following activities.

Author _____

Title _____

Publisher _____ Copyright date _____

1. Briefly describe the PLOT. _____

_____

_____

2. Name the MAIN CHARACTERS and the SUPPORTING CHARACTERS. _____

_____

_____

3. Give the SETTING of the story. _____

_____

4. Give an example of DESCRIPTION from the book. _____

_____

_____

5. Give an example of the DIALOGUE of the main character. _____

_____

Turn in this sheet with the book to be checked. When you have successfully completed this activity, go on to sheet 2-11.

Name _____

Date _____

CONCEPTS OF THE STORY: TEST FRAME

DIRECTIONS: Answer the following questions. As this is a test frame, no answers are given.

1.   Where the story takes place is called the _____.

2.   Whoever is in a story is called a _____.

3.   Whoever is most important is called the _____

_____.

4.   Others in the story who are important are called _____

_____.

5.   The plan of events or what the story is all about is called the _____.

6.   The actual spoken words in a story are enclosed in _____.

7.   How an author tells about someone, or some place, or some thing is called

_____.

8.   The actual spoken words in a story is called the _____.

9.   The three parts of a story are:

_____

_____

_____.

Turn in this test to be corrected. When you have successfully passed this test, go on to sheet 2–12.

Name _____

Date _____

CONCEPTS OF THE STORY: ACTION

ACTION can best be described as the series of events that moves the story along.

When a story moves along at a swift pace, when you cannot put the book down, but want to keep on reading, that story has good action.

When a story seems to drag, when you begin to skim the lines and pages to get to a more interesting part, that story lacks action.

Action does not have to be physical action, the characters do not have to be jumping and bouncing around. Action means that something is always happening, that the story moves along quickly.

DIRECTIONS: Complete the following activities.

1. Choose a book that you have recently read that you feel has lots of action. Tell on the lines below why you feel the book has lots of action.

    Author _____

    Title _____

    Publisher _____   Copyright Date _____

    I feel this book has lots of action because _____

    _____

    _____

    _____

    _____

    _____

Turn in this sheet to be checked. When you have successfully completed this activity, go on to sheet 2–13.

Name _____

Date _____

CONCEPTS OF THE STORY: THEME

Every story has a message, a moral, or an underlying reason for being written.

Usually, this message, moral, or reason is not stated in words. The reader finds out what it is through the story.

This message, moral, or reason contains a common experience that makes it possible for the reader to identify with the characters in the story.

This message, moral, or reason is called the *THEME* of the book.

The *THEME* usually contains a need that the reader is striving to understand or satisfy.

Some examples of *THEME* are:

The need for love   The need for answers to problems

The need for security   The need to belong

The need to know about things   The need to laugh at one's self

The need to achieve   The need to get along with others

DIRECTIONS: Choose two books that you have recently read. Complete the following activities.

BOOK ONE: Author _____

Title _____

Publisher _____ Copyright Date _____

Theme of the book _____

BOOK TWO: Author _____

Title _____

Publisher _____ Copyright Date _____

Theme of the book _____

Turn in this sheet to be checked. When you have successfully completed this sheet, go on to sheet 2–14.

Name _____

Date _____

CONCEPTS OF THE STORY: STYLE

Every author has a distinctive way of selecting and arranging words.

How an author selects and arranges words is called the author's *STYLE*.

An author's *STYLE* is unique to that author and usually cannot successfully be copied.

An author's *STYLE* is the sum total of that author as an individual.

If you like the way a book is written, you probably like that author's style.

If you do not like a book even though the plot is interesting, you probably do not like the author's style.

DIRECTIONS: Choose two books by two different authors that you have recently read. Compare the style of each.

BOOK ONE: Author _____

Title _____

Publisher _____ Copyright Date _____

Author's Style _____

_____

BOOK TWO: Author _____

Title _____

Publisher _____ Copyright Date _____

Author's Style _____

_____

Turn in this sheet to be checked. When you have successfully completed this sheet, go on to sheet 2–15.

Name _____

Date _____

CONCEPTS OF THE STORY: GENRE

Fiction books are sorted into different kinds, types, or categories of stories.

This kind, type, or category of story is called the *GENRE*.

The different *GENRES* include:

Animal	Humorous
Detective	Mystery
Fantasy	Realistic
Historical	Science Fiction

DIRECTIONS: Choose two books you have recently read. Complete the following activities.

BOOK ONE: Author _____

Title _____

Publisher _____ Copyright Date _____

Genre _____

BOOK TWO: Author _____

Title _____

Publisher _____ Copyright Date _____

Genre _____

Turn in this sheet to be checked. When you have successfully completed this sheet, go on to sheet 2–16.

Name _____

Date _____

CONCEPTS OF THE STORY: REVIEW PAGE

ACTION	**STYLE**
THEME	**GENRE**

DIRECTIONS: Cover the answers with your marker. Answer the following questions. Uncover the answers and check your work. Correct if necessary.

1. The series of events that moves the story along is called the

   _____.   action

2. The message, moral, or underlying reason for the book is called the

   _____ of the book.   theme

3. How an author selects and arranges words is called the author's

   _____.   style

4. The kind, type, or category of story is called the

   _____.   genre

5. The need for love and security is one example of a

   _____ of a book.   theme

6. Science fiction is one example of _____.   genre

7. If a story drags in the middle and seems to be going nowhere, that

   story lacks _____.   action

8. Each author has his/her own particular _____   style

   of writing.

9. Humorous fiction is an example of _____.   genre

10. Realistic fiction is an example of _____.   genre

When you feel you have mastered this information, go on to sheet 2–17.

Name _____

Date _____

CONCEPTS OF THE STORY: TEST FRAME

ACTION	**STYLE**
THEME	**GENRE**

DIRECTIONS: Answer the following questions. As this is a test frame, no answers are given.

1. The message, moral, or underlying reason for the book is called the

    _____ of the book.

2. The series of events that moves the story along is called the _____.

3. The kind, type, or category of story is called the _____.

4. The way an author selects and arranges words is called the author's

    _____.

5. Detective fiction is an example of _____.

6. The need to belong and get along with others is an example of a

    _____ of a book.

7. Every author has his/her own particular _____ of writing.

8. A story that moves along quickly shows lots of _____.

9. A mystery fiction is an example of _____.

10. The value of friendship is an example of a _____ of a book.

11. A story that moves slowly lacks _____.

Turn in this sheet to be checked. When you successfully pass this test, you have completed the *Concepts of the Story* Unit.

UNIT 3

Card
Catalog

Name _____

Date _____

UNIT 3: CARD CATALOG
CHECK-OFF SHEET

DIRECTIONS: Below you will find the names of each activity sheet in UNIT 3. Check off each sheet as it is completed.

INTRODUCTION—I 3–1	
INTRODUCTION—II 3–2	
ALPHABETIZING—I 3–3	
ALPHABETIZING—I CONTINUED 3–4	
ALPHABETIZING—II 3–5	
ALPHABETIZING—TEST FRAME 3–6	
AUTHORS 3–7	
ALPHABETIZING AUTHORS 3–8	
SPECIAL RULES 3–9	
TITLES 3–10	
SUBJECTS 3–11	
ALPHABETIZING AUTHORS, TITLES, AND SUBJECTS 3–12	
AUTHORS, TITLES, AND SUBJECTS—TEST FRAME 3–13	
OUTSIDE GUIDES—I 3–14	
OUTSIDE GUIDES—II 3–15	
OUTSIDE GUIDES—III 3–16	
OUTSIDE GUIDES—REVIEW 3–17	
OUTSIDE GUIDES—TEST FRAME 3–18	
CATALOG CARDS—I 3–19	
CATALOG CARDS—II 3–20	
CATALOG CARDS—REVIEW PAGE 3–21	
CATALOG CARDS—TEST FRAME 3–22	
DECODING A CATALOG CARD—I 3–23	
DECODING A CATALOG CARD—II 3–24	
DECODING CATALOG CARDS 3–25	
DECODING A CATALOG CARD—REVIEW PAGE 3–26	
DECODING A CATALOG CARD—TEST FRAME I 3–27	
DECODING A CATALOG CARD—TEST FRAME II 3–28	
LOCATING FICTION BOOKS ON THE SHELF 3–29	
LOCATING PICTURE BOOKS OR EASY BOOKS ON THE SHELF 3–30	
LOCATING NONFICTION BOOKS ON THE SHELF 3–31	
LOCATING BIOGRAPHY BOOKS ON THE SHELF 3–32	
LOCATING BOOKS ON THE SHELF—REVIEW PAGE 3–33	
LOCATING BOOKS ON THE SHELF—TEST FRAME 3–34	
LOCATING BOOKS ON THE SHELF—ACTIVITY PAGE I 3–35	
LOCATING BOOKS ON THE SHELF—ACTIVITY PAGE II 3–36	

Name _____

Date _____

CARD CATALOG: INTRODUCTION—I

The CARD CATALOG tells you what books the library owns.

The CARD CATALOG is the index to the library's collection.

The CARD CATALOG is composed of cards arranged alphabetically in drawers.

The drawers are arranged alphabetically vertically, or up and down—not across.

DIRECTIONS: Cover the answers with your marker. Answer the following questions. Uncover the answers and check your work. Correct if necessary.

1. The card catalog is the _____ to the   index

    library's collection.

2. The card catalog is composed of _____ arranged   cards

    _____ in _____.   alphabetically
                                                     drawers

3. The drawers are arranged _____.   vertically

DIRECTIONS: Answer the following questions.

1. Locate the card catalog in your library.

2. How many drawers are included in the catalog? _____.

When you feel you have mastered this information, go on to sheet 3–2.

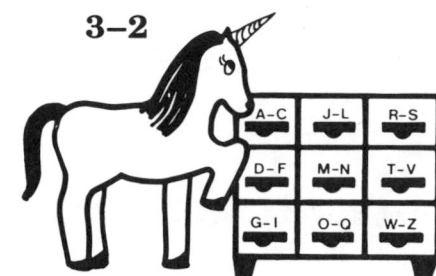

Name _____

Date _____

CARD CATALOG: INTRODUCTION—II

There are three ways to look up a book in the CARD CATALOG.

    1.   By the author's last name.

    2.   By the title of the book.

    3.   By the subject of the book.

DIRECTIONS: Cover the answers with your marker. Answer the following questions. Uncover the answers and check your work. Correct if necessary.

1. One way to look up a book in the card catalog is by the

_____.   author

2. A second way to look up a book is by the _____   title

of the book.

3. A third way to look up a book is by the _____   subject

of the book.

DIRECTIONS: As the card catalog is arranged alphabetically, it is necessary to have a good working knowledge of the alphabet. Write the letters of the alphabet vertically below.

1. ____	6. ____	11. ____	15. ____	19. ____	23. ____
2. ____	7. ____	12. ____	16. ____	20. ____	24. ____
3. ____	8. ____	13. ____	17. ____	21. ____	25. ____
4. ____	9. ____	14. ____	18. ____	22. ____	26. ____
5. ____	10. ____				

When you feel you have mastered this information, go on to sheet 3–3.

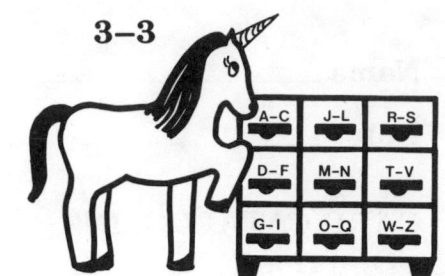

Name _____

Date _____

CARD CATALOG: ALPHABETIZING—I

Practice with the letters that come before and after a letter.

DIRECTIONS: Cover the answers with your marker. Answer the following questions. Uncover the answers and check your work. Correct if necessary.

What letter comes after A? ____			B
What letter comes before B? ____	After B? ____	A	C
What letter comes before C? ____	After C? ____	B	D

What letter comes before D? ____	After D? ____	C	E
What letter comes before E? ____	After E? ____	D	F
What letter comes before F? ____	After F? ____	E	G

What letter comes before G? ____	After G? ____	F	H
What letter comes before H? ____	After H? ____	G	I
What letter comes before I? ____	After I? ____	H	J

What letter comes before J? ____	After J? ____	I	K
What letter comes before K? ____	After K? ____	J	L
What letter comes before L? ____	After L? ____	K	M

Continue on to sheet 3–4.

Name _____

Date _____

CARD CATALOG: ALPHABETIZING—I
CONTINUED

What letter comes before M? ___	After M? ___	L N
What letter comes before N? ___	After N? ___	M O
What letter comes before O? ___	After O? ___	N P
What letter comes before P? ___	After P? ___	O Q
What letter comes before Q? ___	After Q? ___	P R
What letter comes before R? ___	After R? ___	Q S
What letter comes before S? ___	After S? ___	R T
What letter comes before T? ___	After T? ___	S U
What letter comes before U? ___	After U? ___	T V
What letter comes before V? ___	After V? ___	U W
What letter comes before W? ___	After W? ___	V X
What letter comes before X? ___	After X? ___	W Y
What letter comes before Y? ___	After Y? ___	X Z
What letter comes before Z? ___		Y

When you feel you have mastered this information, go on to sheet 3–5.

Name _____

Date _____

CARD CATALOG: ALPHABETIZING—II

Let's practice the letter before and after a letter in mixed-up order.

DIRECTIONS:	Cover the answers with your marker. Write the letter that comes before and after each letter. Uncover the marker and check your work. Correct if necessary.

___ C ___		B	C	D
___ W ___		V	W	X
___ I ___		H	I	J

___ N ___		M	N	O
___ H ___		G	H	I
___ B ___		A	B	C

___ V ___		U	V	W
___ D ___		C	D	E
___ K ___		J	K	L

___ Y ___		X	Y	Z
___ Z ___		Y	Z	
___ Q ___		P	Q	R

___ O ___		N	O	P
___ E ___		D	E	F
___ R ___		Q	R	S

___ U ___		T	U	V
___ L ___		K	L	M
___ F ___		E	F	G

___ T ___		S	T	U
___ J ___		I	J	K
___ X ___		W	X	Y

___ P ___		O	P	Q
___ M ___		L	M	N
___ S ___		R	S	T

| ___ G ___ | | F | G | H |
| ___ A ___ | | | A | B |

When you have mastered this information, go on to sheet 3–6.

Name _____

Date _____

CARD CATALOG: ALPHABETIZING:
TEST FRAME

DIRECTIONS: Write the letter that comes before and after each given letter. As this is a test frame, no answers are given.

1. ___ T ___   14. ___ D ___

2. ___ O ___   15. ___ H ___

3. ___ W ___   16. ___ B ___

4. ___ L ___   17. ___ S ___

5. ___ Y ___   18. ___ E ___

6. ___ J ___   19. ___ X ___

7. ___ A ___   20. ___ P ___

8. ___ V ___   21. ___ C ___

9. ___ N ___   22. ___ U ___

10. ___ Q ___   23. ___ R ___

11. ___ F ___   24. ___ I ___

12. ___ M ___   25. ___ G ___

13. ___ K ___   26. ___ Z ___

Turn in this sheet to be graded. When you have passed the test, go on to sheet 3–7.

Name _____

Date _____

CARD CATALOG: AUTHORS

One way to look up a book in the card catalog is by the author. Authors are listed alphabetically in the card catalog with the last name first.

The *comma* tells you which is the first name and which is the last name.

EXAMPLE: George Scott. No comma. First name, then last name.
George, Scott. Comma. Last name, then first.

If the name contains a middle initial or name, the middle initial or name always follows the first name.

EXAMPLE: James Mason Smith becomes Smith, James Mason
Mary P. White becomes White, Mary P.

DIRECTIONS: Cover the answers with your marker. Answer the following questions. Uncover the answers and check your work. Correct if necessary.

1. Authors are alphabetized in the card catalog with the

    _____ name first.   last

2. The _____ tells you which name is given first.   comma

3. If there is no comma the _____ name is given first.   first

4. If there is a comma, the _____ name is given first.   last

5. A middle initial or name always follows the

    _____ name.   first

When you feel you have mastered this information, go on to sheet 3–8.

Name _____

Date _____

CARD CATALOG: ALPHABETIZING AUTHORS

Authors' names are filed alphabetically in the card catalog by the last name first.

FOR EXAMPLE: Roald Dahl is filed under, *Dahl, Roald.*

Louisa May Alcott is filed under *Alcott, Louisa May.*

DIRECTIONS: Cover the answers with your marker. Alphabetize the following list of authors' names. Uncover the answers and check your work. Correct if necessary.

1. Eleanor Estes _____ Ames, Mildred

2. Zilpha Keatly Snyder _____ Bishop, Curtis

3. Jean Karl _____ Estes, Eleanor

4. Jamie Gilson _____ Gilson, Jamie

5. Mildred Ames _____ Hildick, E. W.

6. Robert Newton Peck _____ Karl, Jean

7. Elizabeth Levy _____ Levy, Elizabeth

8. Jane Yolen _____ Peck, Robert Newton

9. E. W. Hildick _____ Snyder, Zilpha Keatly

10. Curtis Bishop _____ Yolen, Jane

When you feel you have mastered this information, go on to sheet 3–9.

Name _____

Date _____

CARD CATALOG: SPECIAL RULES

Titles are filed alphabetically in the card catalog.

There are special rules for the alphabetical order of titles.

If "A", "An", or "The" appear at the beginning of the title, they are not used. Drop "A", "An", or "The" and alphabetize according to the second word in the title.

EXAMPLE: The title *The Witch's Buttons* is filed under *Witch's Buttons*. The title *A Wrinkle in Time* is filed under *Wrinkle in Time*.

© 1990 by The Center for Applied Research in Education

DIRECTIONS: Cover the answers with your marker. Answer the following questions. Uncover the answers and check your work. Correct if necessary.

1. If _____ appear at the beginning of a title,   A, An, or The

    alphabetize to the second word.

2. To locate the title card for the book, *The Magic of the Glits,*

    drop _____ and alphabetize using   The

    _____.   Magic

3. To locate the title card for the book, *A Tree Is Nice,* drop

    _____ and alphabetize using _____.   A
    Tree

When you feel you have mastered this information, go on to sheet 3–10.

Name _____

Date _____

CARD CATALOG: TITLES

Remember, if "A", "An", or "The" appear at the beginning of a title, alphabetize to the second word.

DIRECTIONS: Cover the answers with your marker. Alphabetize the following list of titles. Uncover your answers and check your work. Correct if necessary.

1. *Ramona the Brave* _____ The Cat in the Hat

2. *The Little House* _____ Curious George

3. *A Wrinkle in Time* _____ Freckle Juice

4. *The Wish Giver* _____ The Little House

5. *Freckle Juice* _____ Ramona the Brave

6. *Curious George* _____ Time of Wonder

7. *The Cat in the Hat* _____ A Tree Is Nice

8. *Time of Wonder* _____ Up a Road Slowly

9. *Up a Road Slowly* _____ The Wish Giver

10. *A Tree Is Nice* _____ A Wrinkle in Time

When you feel you have mastered this information, go on to sheet 3–11.

Name _____

Date _____

CARD CATALOG: SUBJECTS

If you wish to know what the library has on a particular subject, you can look up the subject card.

Subject cards are printed in CAPITAL LETTERS and are filed alphabetically.

DIRECTIONS: Cover the answers with your marker. Alphabetize the following list of subjects. Uncover the answers and check your work. Correct if necessary.

1.	MUSIC	_____	AIRPLANES
2.	POETRY	_____	DINOSAURS
3.	TREES	_____	FISHES
4.	FRUITS	_____	FRUITS
5.	DINOSAURS	_____	HOLIDAYS
6.	OCEAN	_____	MUSIC
7.	FISHES	_____	OCEAN
8.	SPORTS	_____	POETRY
9.	HOLIDAYS	_____	SPORTS
10.	AIRPLANES	_____	TREES

When you feel you have mastered this information, go on to sheet 3–12.

Name _____

Date _____

CARD CATALOG: ALPHABETIZING AUTHORS, TITLES, AND SUBJECTS

In the card catalog, author, title, and subject cards are interfiled alphabetically.

DIRECTIONS: Cover the answers with your marker. Alphabetize the following list of authors, titles, and subjects the way they would appear in the card catalog. Remember to use the special rules for titles. Uncover the answers and check your work. Correct if necessary.

1.	Ezra Jack Keats	_____	Blume, Judy
2.	*The Snowy Day*	_____	*The Cat in the Hat*
3.	*Ramona the Pest*	_____	ELECTRICITY
4.	ELECTRICITY	_____	FISHES
5.	Robert Lawson	_____	*Freckle Juice*
6.	*Many Moons*	_____	*The Glorious Flight*
7.	*A Tree Is Nice*	_____	Keats, Jack Ezra
8.	FISHES	_____	Lawson, Robert
9.	H. A. Rey	_____	*Many Moons*
10.	*The Cat in the Hat*	_____	*Ramona the Pest*
11.	TELEVISION	_____	Rey, H. A.
12.	Judy Blume	_____	*The Snowy Day*
13.	WITCHCRAFT	_____	TELEVISION
14.	*Freckle Juice*	_____	*A Tree Is Nice*
15.	*The Glorious Flight*	_____	WITCHCRAFT

When you feel you have mastered this information, go on to sheet 3–13.

Name _____

Date _____

CARD CATALOG: AUTHORS, TITLES, AND SUBJECTS: TEST FRAME

> DIRECTIONS: Alphabetize the following list of authors, titles, and subjects. Remember to use all the rules you have been learning and practicing. As this is a test frame, no answers are given.

1. DINOSAURS _____

2. Robert Lawson _____

3. POETRY _____

4. *Freckle Juice* _____

5. KANGAROOS _____

6. Jane Yolen _____

7. *Many Moons* _____

8. H. A. Rey _____

9. SPORTS _____

10. *Crow Boy* _____

11. TREES _____

12. *The Biggest Bear* _____

13. C. S. Adler _____

14. NATURAL HISTORY _____

15. *The Wednesday Witch* _____

Turn in this sheet to be graded. When you pass the test, go on to sheet 3–14.

Name _____

Date _____

CARD CATALOG: OUTSIDE GUIDES—I

The card catalog is arranged in alphabetical order in drawers. The outside of the drawers have labels to tell you which letters are included in that drawer. These labels are called the OUTSIDE GUIDES. They guide you to the proper drawer. A small card catalog might look like this.

A – C 1	J – L 4	S – U 7
D – F 2	M – O 5	V – X 8
G – I 3	P – R 6	Y – Z 9

DIRECTIONS: Use the OUTSIDE GUIDES of this card catalog for the activities on sheet 3–15.

Name _____

Date _____

CARD CATALOG: OUTSIDE GUIDES—II

DIRECTIONS: This activity is to be used with the picture of the OUTSIDE GUIDES found on sheet 3–14.

  1. Cover the answers with your marker. In what drawer of the card catalog would the following author, title, and subject cards be found? Write the letters of the drawers on the lines.

  2. Uncover your marker and check your work. Correct if necessary.

  1. Eric Carle   _____   A - C

  2. *Many Moons*   _____   M - O

  3. Jean Karl   _____   J - L

  4. *A Story - A Story*   _____   S - U

  5. *The Biggest Bear*   _____   A - C

  6. Jane Yolen   _____   Y - Z

  7. Ira Waber   _____   Y - Z

  8. POETRY   _____   P - R

  9. *The Finding*   _____   D - F

10. Carolyn Haywood   _____   G -I

11. COOKERY   _____   A - C

12. Elizabeth Levy   _____   J - L

13. *Freckle Juice*   _____   D - F

14. DINOSAURS   _____   D - F

15. *Ramona the Pest*   _____   P - R

When you feel you have mastered this information, go on to sheet 3–16.

Name _____

Date _____

CARD CATALOG: OUTSIDE GUIDES—III

Most card catalogs have the letters of the alphabet divided into more than one drawer. This makes the OUTSIDE GUIDES a bit more complicated to use. You must remember what letters come before and after a given letter.

A larger card catalog might look like this.

Aa – Ann 1	Cr – Dok 7	Gu –He 13	Mas – Mor 19	Sci – Si 25
Anp – Ban 2	Dol – Er 8	Hi – Ho 14	Mos – Ne 20	Ska – Sto 26
Bar – Bl 3	Es – Fe 9	Hu – Ip 15	Ni – Pep 21	Stor – Th 27
Bo – Cap 4	Fi – Fo 10	Ir – Ko 16	Per – Po 22	Ti – Ut 28
Car – Ch 5	Fr – Ge 11	Kr – Lis 17	Pr – Rh 23	V – Wh 29
Ci – Co 6	Gh – Gr 12	Lit – Mar 18	Ri – Sch 24	Wi – XYZ 30

Look carefully at these OUTSIDE GUIDES. If you were looking for an author card for *Beverly Cleary,* you would look first for drawers that have "C" words, then choose *drawer 6* "*Ci - Co*" because the "l" in Cleary comes after the "i" but before the "o."

Use this picture of the card catalog for the activities on sheet 3–17.

Name _____

Date _____

CARD CATALOG: OUTSIDE GUIDES—REVIEW

DIRECTIONS: Cover the answers with your marker. Answer the following questions. Uncover the answers and check your work. Correct if necessary. Use the OUTSIDE GUIDES pictured on the previous page.

EXAMPLE: To locate the title card for the book *Charlie and the Chocolate Factory* you would look in drawer *5 or Car - Ch.*

1. To locate the author card for Roald Dahl, you would look in

   drawer _____.   7 or Cr - Dok

2. To locate a subject card for SCHOOL STORIES, you would

   look in drawer _____.   24 or Ri - Sch

3. To locate the author card for Carolyn Haywood, you would

   look in drawer _____.   13 or Gu - He

4. To locate the title card for *Rabbit Hill,* you would look in

   drawer _____.   23 or Pr - Rh

5. To locate the subject card for AUTOMOBILES, you would

   look in drawer _____.   2 or Anp - Ban

6. To locate the author card for C. S. Adler, you would look in

   drawer _____.   1 or Aa - Ann

7. To locate the title card for *Like Jake and Me,* you would look

   in drawer _____.   17 or Kr - Lis

8. To locate the subject card for WHALES, you would look in

   drawer _____.   29 or V - Wh

When you feel you have mastered this information, go on to sheet 3–18.

Name ———————————————————————

Date ———————————————————————

CARD CATALOG: OUTSIDE GUIDES:
TEST FRAME

DIRECTIONS: This activity is to be used with the picture of the OUTSIDE GUIDES shown on sheet 3–16.

1. In what drawer of the card catalog would the following author, title, or subject cards be found?

2. Please write both the drawer letters and drawer number. As this is a test frame no answers are given.

1. Elizabeth Levy ———————————————————————

2. Jane Yolen ———————————————————————

3. H. A. Rey ———————————————————————

4. Jean Karl ———————————————————————

5. Eric Carle ———————————————————————

6. *Freckle Juice* ———————————————————————

7. *Crow Boy* ———————————————————————

8. *Ramona the Pest* ———————————————————————

9. *The Finding* ———————————————————————

10. *A Story - A Story* ———————————————————————

11. POETRY ———————————————————————

12. COOKERY ———————————————————————

13. MUSIC ———————————————————————

14. DINOSAURS ———————————————————————

15. SPORTS ———————————————————————

Hand in this sheet to be graded. When you pass the test, go on to sheet 3–19.

Name _____

Date _____

CARD CATALOG: CATALOG CARDS—I

There are three main types of catalog cards.

1. Author card
2. Title card
3. Subject card

DIRECTIONS: Cover the answers with your marker. Answer the following questions. Uncover the answers and check your work. Correct if necessary.

The three main types of catalog cards are:

1. _____   author card

2. _____   title card

3. _____   subject card

---

1. All catalog cards begin with the author card. The author's name is on the top line of an author card.

2. To make a title card, the title is added above the author's name.

3. To make a subject card, the subject in CAPITAL LETTERS is added above the author's name.

DIRECTIONS: Cover the answers with your marker. Answer the following questions. Uncover the answers and check your work. Correct if necessary.

1. If the author's name is at the top line of a catalog card, the card is

   an _____ card.   author

2. If the title is at the top line of a catalog card, the card is a

   _____ card.   title

3. If the subject, in CAPITAL LETTERS, is at the top line of a catalog

   card, the card is a _____ card.   subject

When you feel you have mastered this information, go on to sheet 3–20.

Name _____

Date _____

CARD CATALOG: CATALOG CARDS—II

Study carefully the three catalog cards shown below.

1. This is an author card. The top line shows the author's name.

> GAR   Gardiner, John Reynolds
>   Stone fox. Illus by Marcia
> Sewall. Crowell [c1980]
> 85p illus

2. This is a title card for the same book. The top line shows the title of the book.

>   Stone fox
>
> GAR   Gardiner, John Reynolds
>   Stone fox. Illus by Marcia
> Sewall. Crowell [c1980]
> 85p illus

3. This is a subject card for the same book. The top line shows the subject in CAPITAL LETTERS.

>   SLED DOG RACING—FICTION
>
> GAR   Gardiner, John Reynolds
>   Stone fox. Illus by Marcia
> Sewall. Crowell [c1980]
> 85p illus

When you feel you have mastered this information, go on to sheet 3–21.

Name _____

Date _____

CARD CATALOG: CATALOG CARDS: REVIEW PAGE

DIRECTIONS: Cover the answers with your marker. Determine which of the following cards is an author, a title, and a subject card. Write the answer on the line beneath the card. Uncover the answers and check your work. Correct if necessary.

1.

```
          The fun of cooking
641.5     Krementz, Jill
K              The fun of cooking. Knopf
          [c1985]
          117 col illus
```

_____   title card

2.

```
641.5     Krementz, Jill
               The fun of cooking. Knopf
          [c1985]
          117 col illus
```

_____   author card

3.

```
          COOKERY
641.5     Krementz, Jill
               The fun of cooking. Knopf
          [c1985]
          117 col illus
```

_____   subject card

When you feel you have mastered this information, go on to sheet 3–22.

Name _____

Date _____

CARD CATALOG: CATALOG CARDS:
TEST FRAME

DIRECTIONS: Below you will find a selection of author, title, and subject cards. On the line below each card write the type of card. As this is a test frame no answers are given.

SHA   Sharmat, Marjorie Weinman
     Get rich Mitch! Illus by
Loretta Lustig. Morrow
[c1985]
155p illus

_____

LOW   Switcharound
Lowry, Lois
     Switcharound. Houghton
Mifflin. 1985
118p

_____

    STEPFATHERS - FICTION
JUK   Jukes, Mavis
     Like Jake and me. Pictures
by Lloyd Bloom. Knopf [c1984]
unp col illus

_____

CHR   Christopher, Matt
     Supercharged infield.
Illus by Julie Browning.
Little, Brown [c1985]
120p illus

_____

    Quentin Corn
STO   Stoltz, Mary
     Quentin Corn. Illus by Pam-
ela Johnson. Godine [c1984]
121p illus

_____

    MIRRORS - EXPERIMENTS
535   Fitzpatrick, Julie
F   Mirrors. Illus by Sara
Silcock. Silver Burdett
[c1984]

_____

Hand in this test to be graded. When you pass the test, go on to sheet 3-23.

Name _____

Date _____

CARD CATALOG: DECODING A CATALOG CARD—I

A catalog card contains a good deal of information.
A catalog card is arranged in a code or pattern.

When you understand the code or pattern, you can find out a good deal about the book before going to the shelf.

The AUTHOR CARD is the main card.
To make a TITLE CARD, the title is added above the author's name.
To make a SUBJECT CARD, the subject in CAPITAL LETTERS is added above the author's name.

The type of card depends on what is on the top line.
An AUTHOR CARD has the author's name on the top line.
A TITLE CARD has the title on the top line.
A SUBJECT CARD has the subject in CAPITAL LETTERS on the top line.

DIRECTIONS: Cover the answers with your marker. Answer the following questions. Uncover the answers and check your work. Correct if necessary.

1. An author card has the _____   author's name

    on the top line.

2. A title card has the _____   title

    on the top line.

3. A subject card has the _____   subject

    in _____ letters on the top line.   capital

When you feel you have mastered this information, go on to sheet 3–24.

Name _____

Date _____

CARD CATALOG: DECODING A CATALOG CARD—II

The following information is found on a catalog card.

1. Call Number   4. Illustrator   7. Number of Pages

2. Author   5. Publisher

3. Title   6. Copyright Date

Many cards also contain an *ANNOTATION* after the book information.
An *ANNOTATION* tells what the book is about.

DIRECTIONS: Cover the answers with your marker. Answer the following questions. Uncover the answers and check your work. Correct if necessary.

1. The following information will be found on a catalog card.

   1. _____   call number

   2. _____   author

   3. _____   title

   4. _____   illustrator

   5. _____   publisher

   6. _____   copyright date

   7. _____   number of pages

2. The catalog card may contain an

_____ which tells what   annotation

the book is about.

When you feel you have mastered this information, go on to sheet 3–25.

Name _____

Date _____

CARD CATALOG: DECODING CATALOG CARDS

AUTHOR CARD

CALL NUMBER —— 535 —— Fitzpatrick, Julie —— ILLUSTRATOR
AUTHOR —— F —— Mirrors. Illus by Sara —— PUBLISHER
TITLE —— Silcock. Silver-Burdett —— COPYRIGHT
NO. OF PAGES —— [c1984] —— DATE
—— 30p col illus

TITLE CARD

—— Mirrors
CALL NUMBER —— 535 —— Fitzpatrick, Julie —— ILLUSTRATOR
AUTHOR —— F —— Mirrors. Illus by Sara —— PUBLISHER
TITLE —— Silcock. Silver-Burdett —— COPYRIGHT
NO. OF PAGES —— [c1984] —— DATE
—— 30p col illus

SUBJECT CARD

—— MIRRORS - EXPERIMENTS
SUBJECT —— 535 —— Fitzpatrick, Julie —— ILLUSTRATOR
CALL NUMBER —— F —— Mirrors. Illus by Sara —— PUBLISHER
AUTHOR —— Silcock. Silver-Burdett —— COPYRIGHT
TITLE —— [c1984] —— DATE
NO. OF PAGES —— 30p col ilus

When you feel you have mastered this information, use this sheet to answer the questions on sheet 3–26.

Name _____

Date _____

CARD CATALOG: DECODING A CATALOG CARD: REVIEW SHEET

DIRECTIONS: Using the sample set of catalog cards on sheet 3–25, answer the following questions. Uncover the answers and check your work. Correct if necessary.

1. What is the call number for the book?

   _____   535
       F

2. Who is the author of the book?

   _____   Fitzpatrick, Julie

3. What is the title of the book?

   _____   Mirrors

4. Who is the illustrator of the book?

   _____   Sara Silcock

5. Who is the publisher of the book?

   _____   Silver-Burdett

6. What is the copyright date of the book?

   _____   1984

7. How many pages are there in the book?

   _____   30 pages

8. What is the subject of the book?

   _____   MIRRORS - EXPERIMENTS

When you feel you have mastered this information, go on to sheet 3–27.

Name _____

Date _____

CARD CATALOG: DECODING A CATALOG
CARD: TEST FRAME I

DIRECTIONS: Answer the questions concerning each catalog card below. As this is a test frame, no answers are given.

> DEC   DeClements, Berthe
>   6th grade can really kill you.
>   Viking Kestrel [c1985]
>   146p

CALL NUMBER _____ KIND OF CARD _____

AUTHOR _____

TITLE _____

PUBLISHER _____

COPYRIGHT DATE _____ NUMBER OF PAGES _____

> DAH   Charlie and the chocolate factory
>   Dahl, Roald
>   Charlie and the chocolate factory.
>   Illus by Joseph Schindelman. Knopf
>   [c1964]
>   161p illus

CALL NUMBER _____ KIND OF CARD _____

AUTHOR _____

TITLE _____

ILLUSTRATOR _____

PUBLISHER _____

COPYRIGHT DATE _____ NUMBER OF PAGES _____

Continue on to sheet 3-28.

Name _____

Date _____

CARD CATALOG: DECODING A CATALOG CARD:
TEST FRAME II

DIRECTIONS: Answer the questions concerning each catalog card below. As this is a test frame, no answers are given.

> FATHERS - FICTION
> BYA   Byars, Betsy
>   The animal, the vegetable, and
>   John D. Jones. Illus by Ruth
>   Sanderson. Delacorte [c1982]
>   150p illus

CALL NUMBER _____   KIND OF CARD _____

AUTHOR   _____

TITLE   _____

ILLUSTRATOR   _____

PUBLISHER   _____

COPYRIGHT DATE _____   NUMBER OF PAGES _____

> 153.4   Nozaki, Akihiro
> N   Anno's hat tricks. Pictures by
>   Mitsuma Anno. Philomal Bks.
>   [c1985]
>   41p col illus

CALL NUMBER _____   KIND OF CARD _____

AUTHOR   _____

TITLE   _____

ILLUSTRATOR   _____

PUBLISHER   _____

COPYRIGHT DATE _____   NUMBER OF PAGES _____

Hand in this test to be graded. When you pass this test go on to sheet 3-29.

Name _____

Date _____

CARD CATALOG: LOCATING FICTION BOOKS ON THE SHELF

FICTION books are storybooks.

FICTION books have a call number of the first letter or the first three letters of the author's last name.

FOR EXAMPLE: *Freckle Juice* by Judy Blume has a call number of:

  B   or BLU

FICTION books are shelved alphabetically by author in a special section of the library.

DIRECTIONS: Cover the answers with your marker. Answer the following questions. Uncover the answers and check your work. Correct if necessary.

1. FICTION books are _____   storybooks

2. FICTION books have a call number of the

    _____ letter or the first _____   first
    three

    letters of the author's _____ name.   last

3. FICTION books are arranged alphabetically by the author's

    _____ name.   last

4. FICTION books are shelved in a _____   special

    section of the library.

When you feel you have mastered this information, go on to sheet 3–30.

Name _____

Date _____

CARD CATALOG: LOCATING PICTURE BOOKS
OR EASY BOOKS ON THE SHELF

Picture books or Easy books are storybooks.

Picture books or Easy books have a call number of E plus the first letter or the first three letters of the author's last name.

FOR EXAMPLE: Owl Moon by Yolen has a call number of:

E or E
Y Yol

Picture books or Easy books are shelved alphabetically by author in a special section of the library.

DIRECTIONS: Cover the answers with your marker. Answer the following questions. Uncover the answers and check your work. Correct if necessary.

1. Picture books or Easy books are _____.   storybooks

2. Picture books or Easy books have a call number of an

    _____ plus the _____ letter or the first

    E

    first

    three

    _____ letters of the author's _____ name.   last

3. Picture books or Easy books are arranged alphabetically by the

    author's _____ name.   last

4. Picture books or Easy books are shelved in a

    _____ section of the library.   special

When you feel you have mastered this information, go on to sheet 3–31.

Name _____

Date _____

CARD CATALOG: LOCATING NONFICTION BOOKS ON THE SHELF

NONFICTION books are true books of facts.

NONFICTION books have a call number of a number and the first letter or the first three letters of the author's last name.

FOR EXAMPLE: *Tunnels* by Epstein has a call number of:

624   624
    or
  E   EPS

NONFICTION books are arranged on the shelf first by number, then by author letter or letters.

NONFICTION books are shelved in a special section of the library.

DIRECTIONS: Cover the answers with your marker. Answer the following questions. Uncover the answers and check your work. Correct if necessary.

1. NONFICTION books are _____ books   true

   of _____.   facts

2. NONFICTION books have a call number of a _____   number
                                                              letter
   and _____ or _____.   3 letters

3. NONFICTION books are shelved on the shelf first by

   _____ then by _____.   number
                                                              letter

4. NONFICTION books are shelved in a _____   special

   section of the library.

When you feel you have mastered this information, go on to sheet 3-32.

Name _____

Date _____

CARD CATALOG: LOCATING BIOGRAPHY BOOKS ON THE SHELF

There are two types of BIOGRAPHY books.

INDIVIDUAL BIOGRAPHY—about one person
COLLECTIVE BIOGRAPHY—about more than one person

INDIVIDUAL BIOGRAPHY has the call number of:

921 or 92 or B. No author letter is used. This is the only case where an author letter is not used. The letter or three letters under the call number stands for the subject of the book.

FOR EXAMPLE: A book about *Abraham Lincoln* will have L or Lin for Lincoln.
A book about *Sandra Day O'Connor* will have O or O'Co for O'Connor.

COLLECTIVE BIOGRAPHY has a call number of 920 and uses the author letter or first three letters.

DIRECTIONS: Locate the answer to the following question:

1. Circle the call number your library uses for INDIVIDUAL BIOGRAPHY.

      921   92   B

DIRECTIONS: Cover the answers with your marker. Answer the following questions. Uncover the answers and check your work. Correct if necessary.

1. There are two types of BIOGRAPHY books.

_____ and _____ .

    individual
    collective

2. The call letter for individual BIOGRAPHY stands for the

_____ of the book rather than the

    subject

_____ .

    author

When you feel you have mastered this information, go on to sheet 3–33.

Name _____

Date _____

CARD CATALOG: LOCATING BOOKS ON
THE SHELF: REVIEW SHEET

DIRECTIONS: Cover the answers with your marker. Answer the following questions.
Uncover the answers and check your work. Correct if necessary.

1. FICTION books are arranged _____   alphabetically

   on the shelf by the author's _____ name.   last

2. EASY books are arranged _____   alphabetically

   on the shelf by the author's _____ name.   last

3. NONFICTION books are arranged first by

   _____ then by the   number

   author's _____ name.   last

4. BIOGRAPHY books have the call number _____   921
                                                              92
   or _____ or _____ .   B

5. BIOGRAPHY books are not arranged by author, but by the

   subject's _____ name.   last

6. FICTION books are (true) (not true) _____ .   not true

7. NONFICTION books are (true) (not true) _____ .   true

8. EASY books are (true) (not true) _____ .   not true

9. BIOGRAPHY books are (true) (not true) _____ .   true

10. The call number for FICTION is the _____   author

    letter or letters.

11. The call number for NONFICTION is a _____   number

    with the author's letter or letters beneath.

When you feel you have mastered this information, go on to sheet 3–34.

Name _____

Date _____

CARD CATALOG: LOCATING BOOKS ON THE SHELF: TEST FRAME

DIRECTIONS: Answer the following questions. As this is a test frame, no answers are given.

1. FICTION books are arranged _____ on the shelf.

2. FICTION books are arranged by the author's _____ name.

3. E or EASY books are arranged _____ on the shelf.

4. E or EASY books are arranged by the author's _____ name.

5. NONFICTION books are arranged on the shelf first by _____

    then by the author's _____ name.

6. The call number for FICTION is the _____ letter or letters.

7. The call number for E or EASY books is an _____ with the

    _____ letter or letters beneath it.

8. The call number for NONFICTION is a _____ with the

    _____ letter or letters beneath it.

9. The call number for INDIVIDUAL BIOGRAPHY in your library is _____

    _____ with the letter or letters of the _____ beneath it.

10. FICTION books are (true) (not true) _____.

11. NONFICTION books are (true) (not true) _____.

12. E or EASY books are (true) (not true) _____.

13. BIOGRAPHY books are (true) (not true) _____.

Hand in this test to be graded. When you pass the test, go on to sheet 3–35.

Name _____

Date _____

CARD CATALOG: LOCATING BOOKS ON THE SHELF: ACTIVITY PAGE I

DIRECTIONS: This is the final activity for the card catalog unit. This activity consists of locating the book on the shelf.

1. Select a card catalog drawer or use the one assigned to you.

2. A. Find the first nonfiction catalog card. Fill in the information.

    Call Number _____   Author _____

    Title _____

    B. Locate the book on the shelf. Bring it to your seat.
        If the book is not in, locate one with the same call number.

3. A. Find the first fiction catalog card. Fill in the information.

    Call Number _____   Author _____

    Title _____

    B. Locate the book on the shelf. Bring it to your seat.
        If the book is not in, locate one by the same author.

4. A. Find the first E or easy catalog card. Fill in the information.

    Call Number _____   Author _____

    Title _____

    B. Locate the book on the shelf. Bring it to your seat.
        If the book is not in, locate one by the same author.

Continue on to sheet 3–36.

Name _____

Date _____

CARD CATALOG: LOCATING BOOKS ON THE SHELF: ACTIVITY PAGE II

DIRECTIONS: This is the second part of the final activity for the card catalog.

1.   Select a different card catalog drawer or use the one assigned to you.

2.   A.   Find a catalog card with a call number beginning with a 600 number. Fill in the information.

Call Number _____   Author _____

Title _____

   B.   Locate the book on the shelf. Bring it to your seat.
        If the book is not in, locate one with the same call number.

3.   A.   Find a catalog card with a call number beginning with a 700 number. Fill in the information.

Call Number _____   Author _____

Title _____

   B.   Locate the book on the shelf. Bring it to your seat.
        If the book is not in, locate one with the same call number.

4.   A.   Find a catalog card with a call number beginning with an 800 number. Fill in the information.

Call Number _____   Author _____

Title _____

   B.   Locate the book on the shelf. Bring it to your seat.
        If the book is not in, locate one with the same call number.

Turn in this sheet and the books to be checked, then return the book to the book chart. This completes the *Card Catalog* Unit.

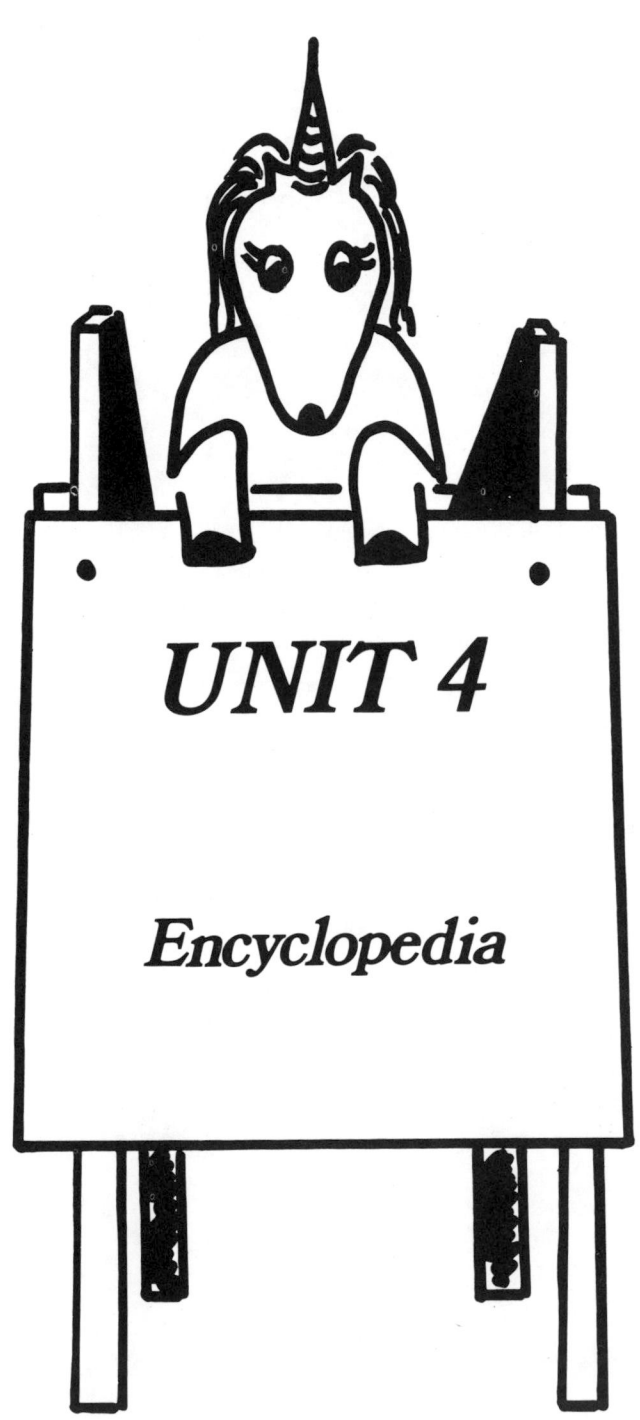

UNIT 4

Encyclopedia

Name _____

Date _____

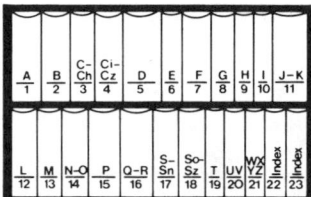

UNIT 4: ENCYCLOPEDIA
CHECK-OFF SHEET

DIRECTIONS: Below you will find the names of each activity sheet in UNIT 4. Check off each sheet as it is completed.

INTRODUCTION 4–1	
ALPHABETICAL ARRANGEMENT 4–2	
IMPORTANT RULES—I 4–3	
IMPORTANT RULES—II 4–4	
REVIEW PAGE 4–5	
TEST FRAME 4–6	
KEY WORDS—I 4–7	
KEY WORDS—II 4–8	
KEY WORDS—REVIEW PAGE 4–9	
KEY WORDS—TEST FRAME 4–10	
GUIDE WORDS—I 4–11	
GUIDE WORDS—II 4–12	
GUIDE WORDS—TEST FRAME 4–13	
CROSS-REFERENCES—I 4–14	
CROSS-REFERENCES—II 4–15	
CROSS-REFERENCES—REVIEW PAGE 4–16	
HEADINGS 4–17	
MAIN HEADINGS AND SUBHEADINGS 4–18	
HEADINGS—REVIEW PAGE 4–19	
CROSS-REFERENCES AND HEADINGS—TEST FRAME 4–20	
PLAGIARISM AND PARAPHRASING 4–21	
USING THE INDEX 4–22	
PLAGIARISM AND PARAPHRASING, USING THE INDEX— REVIEW PAGE 4–23	
PLAGIARISM AND PARAPHRASING, USING THE INDEX— TEST FRAME 4–24	

Name _____

Date _____

ENCYCLOPEDIA: INTRODUCTION

An ENCYCLOPEDIA is a reference book.
A reference book is a book you use to look up or refer to specific information.

EXAMPLE: The telephone book is not usually read from cover to cover.
You look up or refer to a telephone number or address.

The dictionary is not usually read from cover to cover.
You look up or refer to a word in the dictionary.

The telephone book and the dictionary are reference books.

An ENCYCLOPEDIA can be one book, but it is usually a set of books about important people, places, and things.

Each book in a set of books is called a VOLUME.

In an ENCYCLOPEDIA, the volumes are arranged in alphabetical order with each volume containing topics within part of the alphabet.

DIRECTIONS: Cover the answers with your marker. Answer the following questions. Uncover the answers and check your work. Correct if necessary.

1. An encyclopedia is a _____ book.   reference

2. A reference book is a book that you use to _____   look up

   or refer to a topic or subject.

3. An encyclopedia is a set of books about important

   _____, _____,   people
                                                          places

   or _____.   things

4. Each book in an encyclopedia is called a _____.   volume

5. Encyclopedia volumes are arranged in

   _____ order.   alphabetical

When you feel you have mastered this information, go on to sheet 4−2.

Name _____

Date _____

ENCYCLOPEDIA: ALPHABETICAL ARRANGEMENT

There are *two* types of alphabetical arrangement.

1. *UNIT LETTER:* Each volume has all or most of the topics beginning with the same letter in one volume.

    EXAMPLE: The *WORLD BOOK* encyclopedia has unit letter arrangement. Most of the volumes contain a single letter. C and S are divided into two volumes, due to the quantity of topics beginning with C and S.

    J–K, N–O, Q–R, and WXYZ are included together as there are less topics beginning with those letters.

2. *SPLIT LETTER:* Each volume has guide words to show the first and last topic in each volume.

    EXAMPLE: The *MERIT* encyclopedia has split letter arrangement. It is necessary to alphabetize using the guide words on the spines to locate the volume needed.

DIRECTIONS: Locate the encyclopedias in your library. Find examples of UNIT LETTER and SPLIT LETTER arrangement. List the titles below.

1. UNIT LETTER

    a. Title _____

    b. Title _____

2. SPLIT LETTER

    a. Title _____

    b. Title _____

Turn in this sheet to be checked. When you have successfully completed this activity and feel you have mastered this information, go on to sheet 4–3.

Name _____

Date _____

ENCYCLOPEDIA: IMPORTANT RULES—I

| A 1 | B 2 | C– Ch 3 | Ci– Cz 4 | D 5 | E 6 | F 7 | G 8 | H 9 | I 10 | J–K 11 |
| L 12 | M 13 | N–O 14 | P 15 | Q–R 16 | S– Sn 17 | So– Sz 18 | T 19 | UV 20 | WX YZ 21 | Index 22 | Index 23 |

In the ENCYCLOPEDIA, as in all reference books, names of persons are listed by the last name first.

1. Sometimes it is difficult to know whether the first or last name is given first.

2. There is a very easy rule to follow. The *comma* tells you.

EXAMPLE: Scott George. No comma.   Scott is the first name,
George is the last name.

Scott, George. Comma.   Scott is the last name.
George is the first name.

If the name contains a middle initial or a middle name, the middle initial or name always follows the first name.

EXAMPLE: James Mason Smith becomes *Smith, James Mason.*
Betsy C. Maestro becomes *Maestro, Betsy C.*

DIRECTIONS: Cover the answers with your marker. Answer the following questions. Uncover the answers and check your work. Correct if necessary.

1. The _____ tells you which name is given first.   comma

2. If there is no comma, the _____ name is   first

    given first.

3. If there is a comma, the _____ name is   last

    given first.

4. A middle initial or name always follows the _____   first

    name.

When you feel you have mastered this information, go on to sheet 4–4.

Name _____

Date _____

ENCYCLOPEDIA IMPORTANT RULES—II

If the topic contains two or more words, but is not a person's name, look up the topic beginning with the first word.

EXAMPLE: *Valentine's Day.* Do not go to *Day.* Look up using
Valentine's Day.
George Washington Bridge. Do not go to *Washington* or
Bridge. Look up using *George Washington Bridge.*

If the topic has an abbreviation, spell out the word.

EXAMPLE: *No. Carolina.* Spell out *No.* to *North* and look up using
North Carolina.
St. Augustine. Spell out *St.* to *Saint* and look up using
Saint Augustine.

DIRECTIONS:　Cover the answers with your marker. Answer the following questions. Uncover the answers and check your work. Correct if necessary.

1. To locate a topic having two or more words which is not a

   person's name, alphabetize using the _____ 　　　first

   word.

2. To locate the topic, *Thanksgiving Day,* you would look up

   _____. 　　　Thanksgiving
   Day

3. If the topic has an abbreviation, you _____ 　　spell out

   the first word.

4. To locate the topic, *St. Petersburg,* you would look up

   _____. 　　　Saint
   Petersburg

When you feel you have mastered this information, go on to sheet 4–5.

Name _____

Date _____

A 1	B 2	C-Ch 3	Ci-Cz 4	D 5	E 6	F 7	G 8	H 9	I 10	J-K 11
L 12	M 13	N-O 14	P 15	Q-R 16	S-Sn 17	So-Sz 18	T 19	U-V 20	WX YZ 21	Index 22	Index 23

ENCYCLOPEDIA: REVIEW PAGE

DIRECTIONS: Cover the answers with your marker. Answer the following questions. Uncover the answers and check your work. Correct if necessary.

1. An encyclopedia is a _____ book.   reference

2. An encyclopedia contains information about important

   _____, _____,   people
   places

   and _____.   things

3. Each book in a set of books or set of encyclopedias is called a

   _____.   volume

4. Encyclopedias are in _____ order.   alphabetical

5. In reference books, names of persons are listed _____   last

   name first.

6. The _____ tells the order of the name.   comma

7. If there is no comma, the name is given _____   first

   name first.

8. If there is a comma, the name is given _____   last

   name first.

9. If the topic has more than one word, but is not a person, look up

   using the _____ word.   first

© 1990 by The Center for Applied Research in Education

When you feel you have mastered this information, go on to sheet 4–6.

Name _____

Date _____

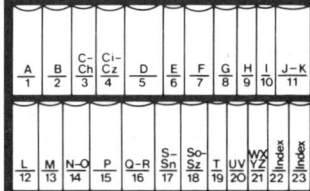

ENCYCLOPEDIA: TEST FRAME

DIRECTIONS: Answer the following questions. As this is a test frame no answers are given.

1. An encyclopedia is a _____ book.

2. A reference book is a book you _____ or refer to

    something in the book.

3. An encyclopedia gives information about important _____,

    _____, and _____.

4. Each book in a set of books is called a _____.

5. Encyclopedias are arranged in _____ order.

6. In reference books, names of persons are listed _____ name first.

7. The _____ tells you the order of the person's name.

8. If there is no comma, the name is listed _____ name first.

9. If there is a comma, the name is listed _____ name first.

10. A person's middle initial or name follows the _____ name.

11. If a topic contains more than one word, but is not a person's name, look up the

    topic _____ word first.

12. If a topic contains an abbreviation, _____ out the abbreviation

    in order to look up the topic.

13. The two kinds of alphabetical arrangement of encyclopedias are called the

    _____ letter and the _____ letter.

Hand in this test to be corrected. When you have passed the test, go on to sheet 4–7.

Name _____

Date _____

ENCYCLOPEDIA: KEY WORDS—I

The word ENTRY is defined as the act of entering.

If you enter a contest, the product you enter is called an ENTRY.

Each topic entered into the encyclopedia is called an ENTRY. The information is the product.

The information written in the encyclopedia about a topic is called an ARTICLE.

Each ENTRY is called a KEY WORD. You look up the KEY WORD to locate the information. Each KEY WORD is printed in dark letters.

© 1990 by The Center for Applied Research in Education

DIRECTIONS: Cover the answers with your marker. Answer the following questions. Uncover the answers and check your work. Correct if necessary.

1. The act of entering is called an _____.   entry

2. The information written in an encyclopedia about a topic is called

   an _____.   article

3. Each entry in an encyclopedia is called a

   _____.   key word

4. You look up the key word to locate the

   _____.   information

5. Each key word is printed in _____   dark

   letters.

When you feel you have mastered this information, go on to sheet 4–8.

Name _____

Date _____

ENCYCLOPEDIA: KEY WORDS—II

A 1	B 2	C-Ch 3	Ci-Cz 4	D 5	E 6	F 7	G 8	H 9	I 10	J-K 11

L 12	M 13	N-O 14	P 15	Q-R 16	S-Sn 17	So-Sz 18	T 19	UV 20	WX YZ 21	Index 22	Index 23

In order to successfully locate the information you seek, you must know what KEY WORD to look up.

If you need to find the answer to the question:

In what state is the Los Alamos National Laboratory located?

You need to:

1. Find out the name of the state.
2. Look up the KEY WORD, Los Alamos National Laboratory, and locate the answer.

DIRECTIONS: Cover the answers with your marker. Underline the KEY WORD in each question. What KEY WORD would you look up to locate the answer? Uncover the marker and check your work. Correct if necessary.

A. 1. What is the population of the city of Chicago? Chicago

2. What do camels eat? camels

3. What is the length of the Nile River? Nile River

4. Who invented the cotton gin? cotton gin

5. In what year was Sandra Day O'Connor born? O'Connor

6. What is the life span of a baboon? baboon

7. What is the name for a baby swan? swan

8. In what country is the city of Paris located? Paris

B. Locate the answer to each question by looking up each KEY WORD. Write the answer to each question on the back of this sheet or on a separate sheet.

Hand in this sheet to be checked. When you have successfully completed this activity, go on to sheet 4-9.

Name _____

Date _____

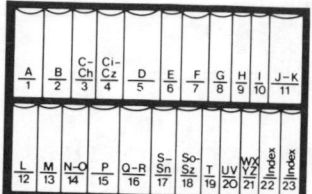

ENCYCLOPEDIA: KEY WORDS: REVIEW SHEET

DIRECTIONS: Cover the answers with your marker. Answer the following questions. Uncover the answers and check your work. Correct if necessary.

1. The act of entering is called an _____.   entry

2. The information written in an encyclopedia about a topic is called

    an _____.   article

3. Each entry in an encyclopedia is called a _____.   key word

4. You look up the key word to locate the _____.   information

5. Each key word is printed in _____ type.   dark

6. What key word would you look up to locate the answer to the

    following question?

    a. Who invented the zipper?   zipper

    b. What is the source of the Hudson River?   Hudson River

    c. In what country was Rudyard Kipling born?   Kipling

When you feel you have mastered this information, go on to sheet 4–10.

Name _____

Date _____

A 1	B 2	C- Ch 3	Ci- Cz 4	D 5	E 6	F 7	G 8	H 9	I 10	J-K 11
L 12	M 13	N-O 14	P 15	Q-R 16	S- Sn 17	So- Sz 18	T 19	UV 20	WX YZ 21	Index 22	Index 23

ENCYCLOPEDIA: KEY WORDS: TEST FRAME

DIRECTIONS: Answer the following questions. As this is a test frame, no answers are given.

1. The act of entering is called an _____.

2. The information written in an encyclopedia about a topic is called an

   _____.

3. Each entry in an encyclopedia is called a _____.

4. You look up the key word to locate the _____.

5. It is necessary to use the right _____ in order to

   locate the information.

6. Each key word is printed in _____ type.

7. What key word would you look up to locate the answer to the following questions?

   a. What is the capital city of Canada?

      Key word _____.

   b. In what year was George Washington born?

      Key word _____.

8. An encyclopedia is arranged in _____ order.

9. Each book in a set of encyclopedias is called a _____.

10. In reference books, names of persons are listed _____ name first.

Hand in this sheet to be graded. When you have successfully passed this test, go on to sheet 4-11.

Name _____

Date _____

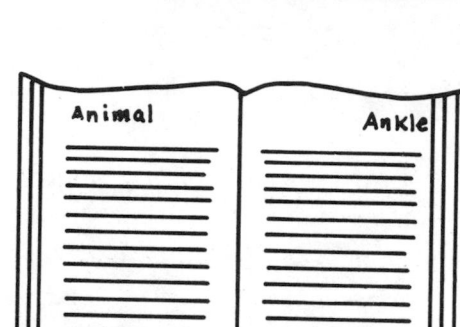

ENCYCLOPEDIA: GUIDE WORDS—I

Reference books have special words at the top of the page to help you locate the information you seek.

These special words are called GUIDE WORDS.

The GUIDE WORD at the top left is the first key word or entry on that page.

The GUIDE WORD at the top right is the last key word or entry on that page.

DIRECTIONS: Cover the answers with your marker. Answer the following questions. Uncover the answers and check your work. Correct if necessary.

1. Reference books have special words at the _____   top

   of the page.

2. These special words are called _____.   guide words

3. These special words are found at the top _____ and   left

   the top _____ of the page.   right

4. The guide word at the top left is the _____   first

   key word or entry.

5. The guide word at the top right is the _____   last

   key word or entry.

When you have mastered this information, select a volume of an encyclopedia. Locate the guide words. Go on to sheet 4–12.

Name _____

Date _____

ENCYCLOPEDIA: GUIDE WORDS—II

GUIDE WORDS guide you to the page needed to locate the information you seek.

If the key word or entry you seek:

1. Comes alphabetically after the GUIDE WORD at the top left, but before the GUIDE WORD at the top right, you will locate the key word or entry on that page or pages.

2. Comes alphabetically before the GUIDE WORD at the top left, you must turn the pages back to locate the proper GUIDE WORD.

3. Comes alphabetically after the GUIDE WORD at the top right, you must turn the pages ahead to locate the proper GUIDE WORD.

DIRECTIONS: Cover the answers with your marker. Answer the following questions. Uncover the answers and check your work. Correct if necessary.

1. Reference books have special words at the top of the pages

   called _____.   guide words

2. In order to locate the proper page, the key word or entry you

   are seeking must come _____ the guide word   after

   on the left and _____ the guide word on the right.   before

3. If the key word or entry does not come between the guide words,

   the key word or entry is _____ on that page.   not

When you have mastered this information, go on to sheet 4–13.

Name _____

Date _____

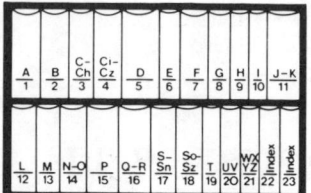

ENCYCLOPEDIA: GUIDE WORDS: TEST FRAME

DIRECTIONS: Answer the following questions. As this is a test frame, no answers are given.

1. Reference books have special words at the _____ of the pages.

2. These special words are called _____.

3. These special words are found at the top _____ and the

    top _____ of the pages.

4. The special word on the left is the _____ word on the page.

5. The special word on the right is the _____ word on the page.

6. These special words help to _____ you to the proper page.

7. If the key word or entry you seek comes before the special word on the left, you

    must turn the pages _____.

8. If the key word or entry you seek comes after the special word on the right, you

    must turn the pages _____.

9. These special words are arranged _____ because

    the encyclopedia is arranged _____.

Hand in this paper to be graded. When you have successfully passed the test, go on to sheet 4–14.

Name _____

Date _____

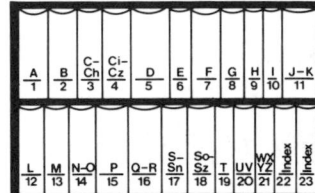

ENCYCLOPEDIA: CROSS-REFERENCES—I

Sometimes the editors of an encyclopedia enter a subject or topic using a different key word or entry than the one you looked up.

The editors must tell you what key word they used.

They use what is called a CROSS-REFERENCE. The CROSS-REFERENCE tells what key word to use.

One code for a CROSS-REFERENCE is "See." When a key word or entry has no information given, you will find the code "SEE," followed by a key word.

EXAMPLE:

> Barn owl. See Owl

When you follow the CROSS-REFERENCE, and you cross over and refer to or look up "owl" rather than Barn owl, you will locate the information.

DIRECTIONS: Locate an encyclopedia volume or use the one assigned to you. Find examples of "SEE" CROSS-REFERENCE.

1. Key word _____

   "See" reference _____

2. Key word _____

   "See" reference _____

3. Key word _____

   "See" reference _____

Hand in this activity to be checked. When you have successfully completed this sheet, go on to sheet 4–15.

Name _____

Date _____

ENCYCLOPEDIA: CROSS-REFERENCES—II

There is a second CROSS-REFERENCE that can help you locate information.

There are times when you may need more than the given information.

At the end of the article, you may find "SEE ALSO," followed by one or more key words.

EXAMPLE:

> See also Mechanical drawing

REMEMBER: "See" tells you there is no information here.
You must follow the CROSS-REFERENCE.

"See also" is located at the end of the article.
Follow the "See also" for more information.

DIRECTIONS: Locate an encyclopedia volume or use the one assigned to you. Find examples of "See also" at the end of articles.

1.   Key word _____

"See also" references _____

2.   Key word _____

"See also" references _____

3.   Key word _____

"See also" references _____

Hand in this sheet to be checked. When you have successfully completed this sheet, go on to sheet 4–16.

Name _____

Date _____

ENCYCLOPEDIA: CROSS-REFERENCES: REVIEW PAGE

A 1	B 2	C- Ch 3	Ci- Cz 4	D 5	E 6	F 7	G 8	H 9	I 10	J-K 11

L 12	M 13	N-O 14	P 15	Q-R 16	S- Sn 17	So- Sz 18	T 19	UV 20	WX YZ 21	Index 22	Index 23

DIRECTIONS: Cover the answers with your marker. Answer the following questions. Uncover the answers and check your work. Correct if necessary.

1. Sometimes information is entered into an encyclopedia under a

   _____ key word or entry.   different

2. You must use a _____ to   cross-
                                                                  reference
   locate the information.

3. A cross-reference means that you _____ over   cross

   and _____ to or look up another subject.   refer

4. The type of cross-reference where you must look up another

   subject is called a _____ reference.   see

5. The type of cross-reference that gives more information is called

   a _____ reference.   see also

6. The _____ reference is located next to the key word or entry.   see

7. The _____ reference is located at the end   see also

   of the article.

When you feel you have mastered this information, go on to sheet 4–17.

Name _____

Date _____

ENCYCLOPEDIA: HEADINGS

The length of an encyclopedia article ranges from a paragraph to many pages.

Sometimes you need a great deal of information. Sometimes you need a short, quick answer.

When the article is long and you need only a quick answer, HEADINGS can help you.

HEADINGS divide a long article into short sections. The HEADING gives the title of each section.

If you check the HEADINGS, you can quickly locate the section that will provide the answer.

DIRECTIONS: Cover the answers with your marker. Answer the following questions. Uncover the answers and check your work. Correct if necessary.

1. An encyclopedia article can range from a _____   paragraph

   to many _____.   pages

2. Long articles are divided into sections through the use of

   _____.   headings
   heading

3. The _____ gives you the _____   title

   of each section.

4. Only _____ articles use headings.   long

5. _____ articles do not need headings.   Short

When you feel you have mastered this information, go on to sheet 4–18.

Name _____

Date _____

ENCYCLOPEDIA: MAIN HEADINGS AND SUBHEADINGS

There are two types of HEADINGS:

MAIN HEADINGS
SUBHEADINGS

MAIN HEADINGS divide a long article into sections.

SUBHEADINGS divide each section into shorter sections.

MAIN HEADINGS are printed in dark type. They are printed in the middle at the head or top of the section.

SUBHEADINGS are printed in dark type, but they are printed at the beginning of the paragraph.

IMPORTANT RULE: If an article has no HEADINGS, read the whole article first.

If an article has HEADINGS, check each MAIN HEADING first.

DIRECTIONS: Locate an encyclopedia volume or use the one assigned to you. Find examples of headings and subheadings.

1. Key word _____

   Main heading _____

   Subheadings _____

   _____

2. Key word _____

   Main heading _____

   Subheadings _____

   _____

When you have mastered this information, go on to sheet 4–19.

Name _____

Date _____

ENCYCLOPEDIA: HEADINGS: REVIEW

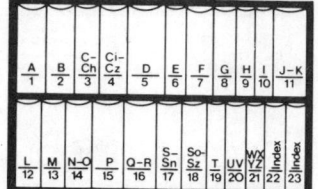

DIRECTIONS: Cover the answers with your marker. Answer the following questions. Uncover the answers and check your work. Correct if necessary.

1. Headings _____ a long article   **divide**

   into short sections.

2. The two types of headings are _____ headings   **main**

   and _____ headings.   **sub**

3. Headings are printed in _____ type.   **dark**

4. The heading that is printed in the middle at the head or top of the

   section is the _____ heading.   **main**

5. The heading that is printed at the beginning of the paragraph is the

   _____ heading.   **sub**

6. Choose an encyclopedia or use the one assigned to you.

   a. Locate *one example* of main headings. List below.

       1. Key word _____

         Main heading _____

   b. Locate *one example* of subheadings. List below.

       1. Key word _____

         Main heading _____

         Subheading _____

When you feel you have mastered this information, go on to sheet 4–20 for cross-references and headings.

Name _____

Date _____

ENCYCLOPEDIA: CROSS-REFERENCES
                   HEADINGS
                   TEST FRAME

A 1	B 2	C-Ch 3	Ci-Cz 4	D 5	E 6	F 7	G 8	H 9	I 10	J–K 11
L 12	M 13	N-O 14	P 15	Q-R 16	S-Sn 17	So-Sz 18	T 19	UV 20	WX YZ 21	Index 22 / Index 23

DIRECTIONS: Answer the following questions. As this is a test frame, no answers are given.

1. The two types of cross-references are _____

   and _____ .

2. The _____ reference tells you there is no information here. You must cross over and refer to a different key word or words.

3. The _____ reference is located at the end of the article to give extra information.

4. Headings _____ a long article into short sections.

5. The two types of headings are _____ headings and _____ headings.

6. Headings are printed in _____ type.

7. The _____ heading is printed in the middle at the head or top of the section.

8. The _____ heading is printed at the beginning of the paragraph.

Hand in this test to be graded. When you have successfully passed the test, go on to sheet 4–21.

| A 1 | B 2 | C- Ch 3 | Ci- Cz 4 | D 5 | E 6 | F 7 | G 8 | H 9 | I 10 | J-K 11 |
| L 12 | M 13 | N-O 14 | P 15 | Q-R 16 | S- Sn 17 | So- Sz 18 | T 19 | U-V 20 | W-X Y-Z 21 | Index 22 | Index 23 |

ENCYCLOPEDIA: PLAGIARISM AND PARAPHRASING

It is against the law to copy copyrighted material.

Copying copyrighted material is called PLAGIARISM.

However, encyclopedias and other reference tools contain information that is meant for you to use in research and writing reports.

What do you do?

You PARAPHRASE the information. You may copy the facts, but you must express in your own words and sentence structure the meaning of the facts. PARAPHRASING is not easy. It requires practice.

DIRECTIONS: Cover the answers with your marker. Answer the following questions. Uncover the answers and check your work. Correct if necessary.

1. It is against the _____ to copy   law

   copyrighted materials.

2. Copying copyrighted materials is called

   _____.   plagiarism

3. Because you cannot copy the material, you

   _____ the material.   paraphrase

4. You copy the _____.   facts

5. You express in your own words the _____   meaning

   of the material.

6. Paraphrasing requires _____.   practice

When you feel you have mastered this information, go on to sheet 4–22.

Name _____

Date _____

ENCYCLOPEDIA: USING THE INDEX

Most encyclopedia sets include an INDEX.

The INDEX is an alphabetical listing of all topics or entries included in the set.

Usually, the INDEX is the last or final volume or is included in the final volume. Occasionally the INDEX is the first volume.

In order to obtain all possible information, it is important to use the INDEX.

The INDEX gives the volume and page of all the information on a topic or subject. If you use only the volume containing the key word or entry, you may miss important information.

INDEX
22

DIRECTIONS: Cover the answers with your marker. Answer the following questions. Uncover the answers and check your work. Correct if necessary.

1. The _____ is listed alphabetically.   index

2. The index is usually located in the _____   final

   volume of the set.

3. The index gives the _____ and   volume

   _____ of all information on a topic or subject.   page

4. If you do not use the index, you may _____   miss

   important information.

When you feel you have mastered this information, go on to sheet 4–23.

Name _____

Date _____

A 1	B 2	C– Ch 3	Ci– Cz 4	D 5	E 6	F 7	G 8	H 9	I 10	J–K 11
L 12	M 13	N–O 14	P 15	Q–R 16	S– Sn 17	So– Sz 18	T 19	U V 20	W X Y Z 21	Index 22	Index 23

ENCYCLOPEDIA: PLAGIARISM AND PARAPHRASING, USING THE INDEX: REVIEW SHEET

DIRECTIONS: Cover the answers with your marker. Answer the following questions. Uncover the answers and check your work. Correct if necessary.

1. It is against the law to _____ copyrighted materials.
           copy

2. To do so is called _____.
           plagiarism

3. Rather than copy the material, you _____ the material.
           paraphrase

4. You may copy the _____.
           facts

5. Paraphrasing means to express the meaning of the information in your own _____.
           words

6. Most encyclopedias include an _____.
           index

7. The index is usually located in the _____ volume of the set.
           final

8. Each entry in the index contains the _____ and _____ where the information will be found.
           volume
           page

9. If you do not use the index, you may _____ important information.
           miss

When you feel you have mastered this information, go on to sheet 4–24.

Name _____

Date _____

ENCYCLOPEDIA: PLAGIARISM AND PARAPHRASING
USING THE INDEX
TEST FRAME

A 1	B 2	C-Ch 3	Ci-Cz 4	D 5	E 6	F 7	G 8	H 9	I 10	J-K 11

L 12	M 13	N-O 14	P 15	Q-R 16	S-Sn 17	So-Sz 18	T 19	UV 20	WX YZ 21	Index 22	Index 23

DIRECTIONS: Answer the following questions. As this is a test frame, no answers are given.

1. It is against the law to _____ copyrighted material.

2. Copying copyrighted material is called _____.

3. Because you cannot copy copyrighted material, you _____ the material.

4. You can copy the _____.

5. You express in your own words the _____ of the material.

6. The index is listed _____.

7. The index is usually located in the _____ volume of the encyclopedia set.

8. The index gives you the _____ and _____ number of all information on a topic.

9. When you do not bother to use the index, you may _____ important information.

Hand in this test to be graded. When you successfully pass this test you have completed the *Encyclopedia* Unit.

UNIT 5

Dewey Decimal Classification System

Name _____

Date _____

UNIT 5: DEWEY DECIMAL CLASSIFICATION SYSTEM CHECK-OFF SHEET

DIRECTIONS: Below you will find the names of each activity sheet in UNIT 5. Check off each sheet as it is completed.

INTRODUCTION 5–1	
ACTIVITY PAGE 5–2	
DECIMAL SYSTEM 5–3	
REVIEW PAGE 5–4	
TEST FRAME 5–5	
MAIN CLASSES 5–6	
PRACTICE WITH THE MAIN CLASSES—000—100s 5–7	
PRACTICE WITH THE MAIN CLASSES—200—300s 5–8	
PRACTICE WITH THE MAIN CLASSES—400—500s 5–9	
PRACTICE WITH THE MAIN CLASSES—600—700s 5–10	
PRACTICE WITH THE MAIN CLASSES—800—900s 5–11	
PRACTICE WITH DEWEY 5–12	
PRACTICE WITH DEWEY CONTINUED 5–13	
PRACTICE WITH DEWEY CONTINUED 5–14	
MORE PRACTICE WITH DEWEY 5–15	
MORE PRACTICE WITH DEWEY CONTINUED 5–16	
PRACTICE WITH THE MAIN CLASSES: REVIEW 5–17	
TEST FRAME 5–18	

Name _____

Date _____

000 General work
100 Philosophy
200 Religion
300 Social Science
400 Language
500 Science
600 Applied Science
700 Fine Arts
800 Literature

THE DEWEY DECIMAL CLASSIFICATION SYSTEM: INTRODUCTION

THE DEWEY DECIMAL CLASSIFICATION SYSTEM was designed by Melvil Dewey in 1876.

Up to that time, each library had its own system of organizing and arranging books.

Melvil Dewey worked in the library while attending Amherst College in Massachusetts. He felt that if nonfiction books were arranged on the shelf by subject, books on the same subject would be shelved together.

Melvil Dewey divided all of knowledge into ten main classes.

DIRECTIONS: Cover the answers with your marker. Answer the following questions. Uncover the answers and check your work. Correct if necessary.

1. The Dewey Decimal Classification was designed by

    _____.   Melvil Dewey

2. Up to that point, each library had its own system for

    _____ and   organizing

    _____ books.   arranging

3. Dewey felt that if nonfiction books were arranged by

                                                                 subject
    _____, books on the same _____   subject

    would be shelved together.

4. Dewey divided all of knowledge into _____ main   ten

    classes.

When you feel you have mastered this information, go on to sheet 5–2.

Name _____

Date _____

THE DEWEY DECIMAL CLASSIFICATION
SYSTEM: ACTIVITY PAGE

000 General
100 Philosophy
200 Religion
300 Social Science
400 Language
500 Science
600 Applied Science
700 Fine Arts
800 Literature

DIRECTIONS: Look up Melvil Dewey in an encyclopedia. Complete the following
activities.

1. Date of birth _____

    Place of birth _____

2. Date of graduation from Amherst College _____

3. Contributions other than designing the Dewey Decimal Classification System

    _____

    _____

    _____

    _____

    _____

    _____

    _____

    _____

    _____

    _____

    _____

    Date of death _____

Hand in this sheet to be checked. When you have successfully completed this activity, go on
to sheet 5–3.

Name _____

Date _____

THE DEWEY DECIMAL CLASSIFICATION SYSTEM: DECIMAL SYSTEM

The Dewey Decimal Classification System
is based on the number ten.

The Dewey Decimal Classification has ten
main classes. Each class has ten divisions
and each division has ten divisions, and so
on to the individual number for each subject.

The DEWEY DECIMAL CLASSIFICATION SYSTEM
also uses the first letter or the first three letters of the
author's last name. This letter or letters is located under the
number. This combination, known as the CALL NUMBER,
is found:

a. On the catalog card   c. On the book card

b. On the book's spine   d. On the book pocket

DIRECTIONS: Cover the answers with your marker. Answer the following questions.
Uncover the answers and check your work. Correct if necessary.

1. The Dewey Decimal Classification System is based on the

   number _____.   ten

2. The Dewey Decimal Classification System uses a

   _____ as well as the number. This   letter

   combination is known as the _____.   call number

3. This combination is found in four places.

   _____   _____   catalog card
                                                                    books's spine
   _____   _____   book card
                                                                    book pocket

---

When you feel you have mastered this information, go on to sheet 5–4.

Name _____

Date _____

THE DEWEY DECIMAL CLASSIFICATION SYSTEM: REVIEW PAGE

```
000 General
100 Philosophy
200 Religion
300 Social Science
400 Language
500 Science
600 Applied Science
700 Fine Arts
800 Literature
```

DIRECTIONS: Cover the answers with your marker. Answer the following questions. Uncover the answers and check your work. Correct if necessary.

1. The Dewey Decimal Classification System was designed by

_____.   Melvil Dewey

2. The Dewey Decimal Classification has _____   ten

main classes.

3. The Dewey Decimal Classification System is based on the

number _____.   ten

4. The Dewey Decimal Classification System uses a

_____ as well as a number. This combination   letter

is known as the _____.   call number

5. This combination is found in four places:

_____   catalog card

_____   book s spine

_____   book card

_____   book pocket

6. The Dewey Decimal Classification System is used for

_____ books.   nonfiction

When you feel you have mastered this information, go on to sheet 5–5.

Name _____

Date _____

THE DEWEY DECIMAL CLASSIFICATION SYSTEM: TEST FRAME

000 General
100 Philosophy
200 Religion
300 Social Science
400 Language
500 Science
600 Applied Science
700 Fine Arts
800 Literature

DIRECTIONS: Answer the following questions. As this is a test frame, no answers are given.

1. The Dewey Decimal Classification System was designed by

   _____.

2. The Dewey Decimal Classification System is used for

   _____ books.

3. The Dewey Decimal Classification System has

   _____ main classes.

4. The Dewey Decimal Classification is based on the number

   _____.

5. Through use of The Dewey Decimal Classification, books on the same

   _____ are shelved together.

6. The Dewey Decimal Classification System uses a _____

   as well as a number.

7. This combination is known as the _____.

8. This combination is found in four places:

   _____

   _____

   _____

   _____

Hand in this sheet to be graded. When you successfully pass the test, go on to sheet 5–6.

© 1990 by The Center for Applied Research in Education

Name _____

Date _____

THE DEWEY DECIMAL CLASSIFICATION SYSTEM: MAIN CLASSES

There are ten main classes in the Dewey Decimal Classification System.

000 General Works
100 Philosophy and Psychology
200 Religion
300 Social Science
400 Language

500 Science
600 Applied Science and Technology
700 Fine Arts and Recreation
800 Literature
900 Geography, History, and Biography

DIRECTIONS: Cover the answers with your marker. Answer the following questions. Uncover the answers and check your work.

1. Books on Religion have a number in the _____. 200s

2. Books on Science have a number in the _____. 500s

3. Books on Fine Arts and Recreation have a number in the

   _____. 700s

4. Books on Literature have a number in the _____. 800s

5. Books on Language have a number in the _____. 400s

6. Books on General Works have a number in the _____. 000s

7. Books on Geography, History, and Biography have a number in

   the _____. 900s

8. Books on Social Science have a number in the _____. 300s

9. Books on Philosophy and Psychology have a number in the

   _____. 100s

10. Books on Applied Science and Technology have a number in

    the _____. 600s

When you feel you have mastered this information, go on to sheet 5–7.

Name _____

Date _____

THE DEWEY DECIMAL CLASSIFICATION SYSTEM: PRACTICE WITH THE MAIN CLASSES

000 General Work
100 Philosophy a
200 Religion
300 Social Scienc
400 Language
500 Science
600 Applied Science
700 Fine Arts
Literature

000 - 099 General Works

Materials that are not restricted to one subject but contain more than one subject within the whole, such as encyclopedias, magazines, newspapers.

100 - 199 Philosophy and Psychology

Materials that contain information on man's thoughts and ideas.

DIRECTIONS: For this activity, you must have access to the nonfiction shelves. Complete the following activities.

1. Locate the shelving for books and other materials with a number of between 000 - 099. Discover the individual subjects in this main class through browsing through the titles and the books. Write down as many individual subjects as you can find.

   _____

   _____

   _____

2. Locate the shelving for books and other materials with a number of between 100 - 199. Discover the individual subjects in this main class through browsing through the titles and the books. Write down as many individual subjects as you can find.

   _____

   _____

   _____

Hand in this sheet to be checked. When you have successfully completed this activity, go on to sheet 5–8.

Name _____

Date _____

THE DEWEY DECIMAL CLASSIFICATION SYSTEM: PRACTICE WITH THE MAIN CLASSES

(unicorn thought bubble:)
000 General work
100 Philosophy
200 Religion
300 Social Science
400 Language
500 Science
600 Applied Science
700 Fine Arts
800 Literature

200 - 299 Religion

   Materials that contain information on the various beliefs of peoples.

300 - 399 Social Science

   Materials that contain information on people living and working together.

DIRECTIONS: Complete the following activities.

1. Locate the shelving for books and other materials with a number of between 200 - 299. Discover the individual subjects in this main class through browsing through the titles and the books. Write down as many individual subjects as you can find.

   _____

   _____

   _____

2. Locate the shelving for books and other materials with a number of between 300 - 399. Discover the individual subjects in this main class through browsing through the titles and the books. Write down as many individual subjects as you can find.

   _____

   _____

   _____

Hand in this sheet to be checked. When you have successfully completed this activity, go on to sheet 5–9.

Name _____

Date _____

THE DEWEY DECIMAL CLASSIFICATION SYSTEM: PRACTICE WITH THE MAIN CLASSES

400 - 499 Language

   Materials that contain information on all the languages of the world.

500 - 599 Science

   Materials that contain information on the various aspects of pure science.

DIRECTIONS: Complete the following activities.

1. Locate the shelving for books and other materials with a number of between 400 - 499. Discover the individual subjects in this main class through browsing through the titles and the books. Write down as many individual subjects as you can find.

   _____

   _____

   _____

2. Locate the shelving for books and other materials with a number of between 500 - 599. Discover the individual subjects in this main class through browsing through the titles and the books. Write down as many individual subjects as you can find.

   _____

   _____

   _____

Hand in this sheet to be checked. When you have successfully completed this activity, go on to sheet 5–10.

Name _____

Date _____

THE DEWEY DECIMAL CLASSIFICATION SYSTEM: PRACTICE WITH THE MAIN CLASSES

600 - 699 Applied Science and Technology

Materials that contain information on the applications of science.

700 - 799 Fine Arts and Recreation

Materials that contain information on how people use their creativity and their free time.

DIRECTIONS: Complete the following activities.

1. Locate the shelving for books and other materials with a number of between 600 - 699. Discover the individual subjects in this main class through browsing through the titles and the books. Write down as many individual subjects as you can find.

   _____

   _____

   _____

2. Locate the shelving for books and other materials with a number of between 700 - 799. Discover the individual subjects in this main class through browsing through the titles and the books. Write down as many individual subjects as you can find.

   _____

   _____

   _____

Hand in this sheet to be checked. When you have successfully completed this activity, go on to sheet 5–11.

Name _____

Date _____

THE DEWEY DECIMAL CLASSIFICATION SYSTEM: PRACTICE WITH THE MAIN CLASSES

800 - 899 Literature

Materials that contain collections and information on all types of literature.

900 - 999 Geography, History, and Biography

Materials that contain information on places, events, and famous people.

DIRECTIONS: Complete the following activities.

1. Locate the shelving for books and other materials with a number of between 800 - 899. Discover the individual subjects in this main class through browsing through the titles and the books. Write down as many individual subjects as you can find.

    _____

    _____

    _____

2. Locate the shelving for books and other materials with a number of between 900 - 999. Discover the individual subjects in this main class through browsing through the titles and the books. Write down as many individual subjects as you can find.

    _____

    _____

    _____

Hand in this sheet to be checked. When you have successfully completed this activity go on to sheet 5–12.

Name _____

Date _____

THE DEWEY DECIMAL CLASSIFICATION SYSTEM: PRACTICE WITH DEWEY

000 General Work
100 Philosophy
200 Religion
300 Social Science
400 Language
500 Science
600 Applied Science
700 Fine Arts
800 Literature

DIRECTIONS: For this activity you must have access to the nonfiction shelves. Complete the following activities.

1. Locate a nonfiction book with the Dewey number 001.64.

   A. Author _____

   B. Title _____

   C. Subject of book _____

   D. Are there other books on the same subject? _____

2. Locate a nonfiction book with the Dewey number 152.4.

   A. Author _____

   B. Title _____

   C. Subject of book _____

   D. Are there other books on the same subject? _____

3. Locate a nonfiction book with the Dewey number 292.

   A. Author _____

   B. Title _____

   C. Subject of book _____

   D. Are there other books on the same subject? _____

Continue on to sheet 5–13.

PRACTICE WITH DEWEY (CONTINUED)

000 General work
100 Philosophy
200 Religion
300 Social Science
400 Language
500 Science
600 Applied Science
700 Fine Arts
800 Literature

4. Locate a nonfiction book with the Dewey number 398.

   A. Author _____

   B. Title _____

   C. Subject of book _____

   D. Are there other books on the same subject? _____

5. Locate a nonfiction book with the Dewey number 448.6.

   A. Author _____

   B. Title _____

   C. Subject of book _____

   D. Are there other books on the same subject? _____

6. Locate a nonfiction book with the Dewey number 598.2.

   A. Author _____

   B. Title _____

   C. Subject of book _____

   D. Are there other books on the same subject? _____

7. Locate a nonfiction book with the Dewey number 629.4.

   A. Author _____

   B. Title _____

   C. Subject of book _____

   D. Are there other books on the same subject? _____

Hand in this activity to be checked. Go on to sheet 5–14.

Name _____

Date _____

PRACTICE WITH DEWEY (CONTINUED)

000 General
100 Philosophy
200 Religion
300 Social Science
400 Language
500 Science
600 Applied Science
700 Fine Arts
800 Literature

8. Locate a nonfiction book with the Dewey number 796.4.

   A. Author _____

   B. Title _____

   C. Subject of book _____

   D. Are there other books on the same subject? _____

9. Locate a nonfiction book with the Dewey number 811.

   A. Author _____

   B. Title _____

   C. Subject of book _____

   D. Are there other books on the same subject? _____

10. Locate a nonfiction book with the Dewey number 973.

    A. Author _____

    B. Title _____

    C. Subject of book _____

    D. Are there other books on the same subject? _____

11. Locate a nonfiction book with the Dewey number 921 or 92 or B.

    A. Author _____

    B. Title _____

    C. Subject of book _____

    D. Are there other books on the same subject? _____

Hand in this activity to be checked. Go on to sheet 5–15.

Name _____

Date _____

THE DEWEY DECIMAL CLASSIFICATION SYSTEM: MORE PRACTICE WITH DEWEY

000 General
100 Philosophy
200 Religion
300 Social Science
400 Language
500 Science
600 Applied Science
700 Fine Arts
Literature

DIRECTIONS: How many subjects can you think of in each Dewey main class listed below? Write the subjects on the lines below.

1. 000 - 099

    _____

    _____

2. 100 - 199

    _____

    _____

3. 200 - 299

    _____

    _____

4. 300 - 399

    _____

    _____

5. 400 - 499

    _____

    _____

6. 500 - 599

    _____

    _____

Continue on to sheet 5–16.

Name _____

Date _____

THE DEWEY DECIMAL CLASSIFICATION SYSTEM: MORE PRACTICE WITH DEWEY (CONTINUED)

000 General
100 Philosophy
200 Religion
300 Social Science
400 Language
500 Science
600 Applied Science
700 Fine Arts
800 Literature

DIRECTIONS: How many subjects can you think of in each Dewey main class listed below? Write the subjects on the lines below.

7. 600 - 699

_____

_____

8. 700 - 799

_____

_____

9. 800 - 899

_____

_____

10. 900 - 999

_____

_____

11. 921, 92 or B

_____

_____

Hand in this sheet to be checked. When you have successfully completed this activity, go on to sheet 5–17.

Name _____

Date _____

THE DEWEY DECIMAL CLASSIFICATION SYSTEM: PRACTICE WITH MAIN CLASSES: REVIEW PAGE

000 General Works
100 Philosophy and Psychology
200 Religion
300 Social Science
400 Language

500 Science
600 Applied Science and Technology
700 Fine Arts and Recreation
800 Literature
900 Geography, History, and Biography

DIRECTIONS: Cover the answers with your marker. Using the main classes listed above, assign the main class number and name to the subjects below. Uncover the answers and check your work. Correct if necessary.

EXAMPLE:

1.	Baseball	700	Fine Arts & Recreation	
2.	Ants	_____	_____	500 Science
3.	Greek Myths	_____	_____	200 Religion
4.	Poetry	_____	_____	800 Literature
5.	Canada	_____	_____	900 Geo., Hist., & Bio.
6.	French	_____	_____	400 Language
7.	Civil War	_____	_____	900 Geo., Hist., & Bio.
8.	Space Travel	_____	_____	600 App. Sci. & Tech.
9.	Emotions	_____	_____	100 Phil. & Psych.
10.	Encyclopedias	_____	_____	000 General Works
11.	Prayers	_____	_____	200 Religion
12.	Government	_____	_____	300 Social Science
13.	Dance	_____	_____	700 Fine Arts & Rec.
14.	Dreams	_____	_____	100 Phil. & Psych.

When you feel you have mastered this information, go on to sheet 5–18.

Name _____

Date _____

THE DEWEY DECIMAL CLASSIFICATION
SYSTEM: TEST FRAME

DIRECTIONS: Assign a main class Dewey number to the following subjects. As this is a test frame, no answers are given.

1. Football _____

2. Snakes _____

3. Sign Language _____

4. The Bible _____

5. Newspapers _____

6. Feelings _____

7. Poetry _____

8. Airplanes _____

9. Revolutionary War _____

10. Electricity _____

11. Swimming _____

12. Italian Language _____

13. Drawing _____

14. United States _____

15. Dinosaurs _____

16. Magazines _____

17. Hockey _____

Hand in this test to be graded. When you have successfully passed the test, you have completed the Unit.

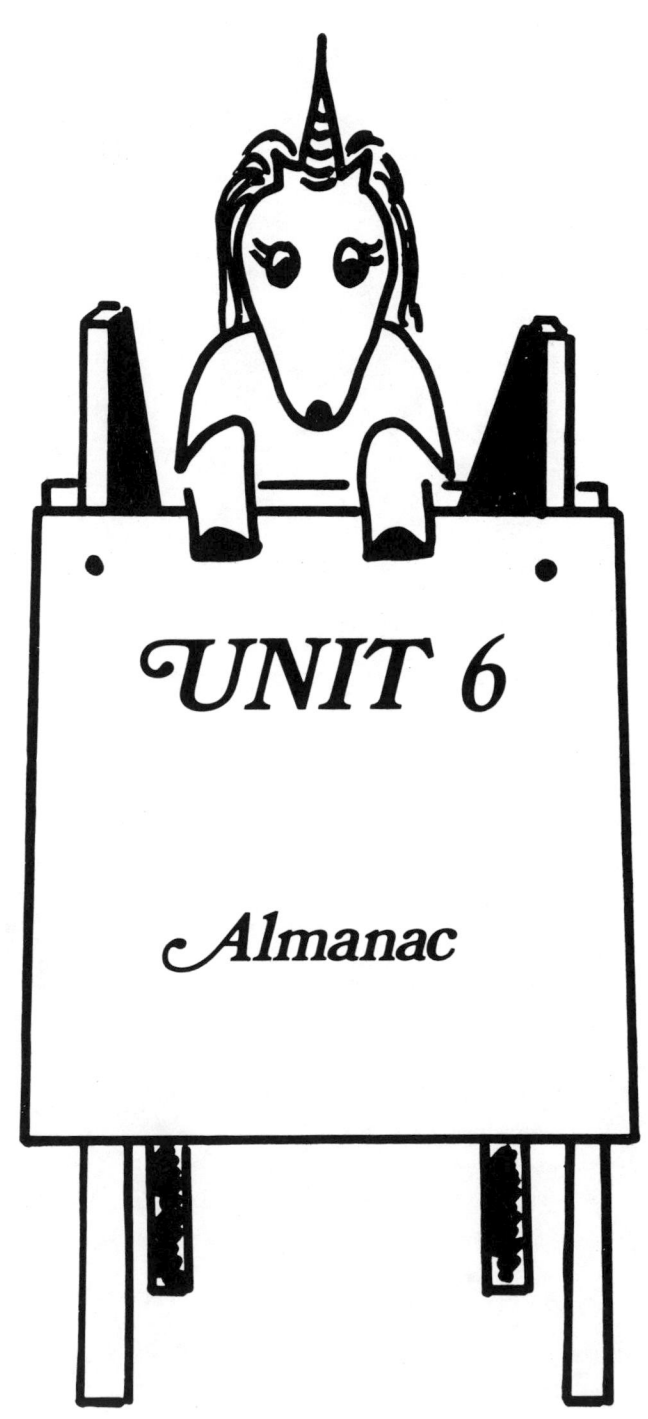

UNIT 6

Almanac

Name _____

Date _____

UNIT 6: ALMANAC
CHECK-OFF SHEET

DIRECTIONS: Below you will find the names of each activity sheet in UNIT 6. Check off each sheet as it is completed.

INTRODUCTION 6–1	
THE WORLD ALMANAC AND BOOK OF FACTS 6–2	
REVIEW SHEET 6–3	
TEST FRAME 6–4	
USING THE INDEX 6–5	
PRACTICE WITH *THE WORLD ALMANAC* 6–6	
PRACTICE USING *THE WORLD ALMANAC* 6–7	

Name _____

Date _____

ALMANAC: INTRODUCTION

An ALMANAC is a book containing a calendar and statistics about people, places, and things.

An ALMANAC is published yearly.

An ALMANAC contains information in such fields as:

Art	Geography	Literature
Drama	Government	Science
Economics	History	Sports

An ALMANAC provides current up-to-date information.

DIRECTIONS: Cover the answers with your marker. Answer the following questions. Uncover the answers and check your work. Correct if necessary.

1. An almanac is a book containing a calendar and statistics about

   _____, _____,

   and _____.

2. An almanac is published _____.

3. An almanac provides current _____ information.

people
places
things

yearly

up-to-date

DIRECTIONS: Locate the almanac or almanacs available in your library. What is the latest edition?

1. Title _____ Year _____

2. Title _____ Year _____

When you feel you have mastered this information, go on to sheet 6–2.

Name _____

Date _____

ALMANAC: *THE WORLD ALMANAC AND BOOK OF FACTS*

A well-known ALMANAC is *THE WORLD ALMANAC AND BOOK OF FACTS*, better known as *THE WORLD ALMANAC*.

THE WORLD ALMANAC is published annually in November.

THE WORLD ALMANAC contains more than 1 million facts in such fields as:

Astronomy	Nations
Awards	Personalities
Current Events	Population
Economics	Sports
Geography	Vital Statistics

The index to *THE WORLD ALMANAC* is located in the front of the book.

DIRECTIONS: Cover the answers with your marker. Answer the following questions. Uncover the answers and check your work. Correct if necessary.

1. A well-known almanac is *The* _____   *World*

   Almanac and Book of Facts.

2. *The World Almanac* is published annually in

   _____.   November

3. *The World Almanac* contains more than 1 _____   million

   facts and figures.

4. The index to *The World Almanac* is located in the

   _____ of the book.   front

When you feel you have mastered this information, go on to sheet 6–3.

Name _____

Date _____

ALMANAC: INTRODUCTION: REVIEW PAGE

DIRECTIONS: Cover the answers with your marker. Answer the following questions. Uncover the answers and check your work. Correct if necessary.

1. An almanac is a book containing information about

   _____, _____,

   and _____.

2. An almanac is published _____.

3. An almanac provides _____

   up-to-date information.

4. A well-known almanac is _____

   _____.

5. *The World Almanac* is published annually in

   _____.

6. *The World Almanac* contains more than 1 _____

   facts and figures.

7. The index to *The World Almanac* is located in the _____

   of the book.

8. The index to *The World Almanac* is listed in

   _____ order.

people
places

things

yearly

current

*The
World
Almanac*

November

million

front

alphabetical

When you feel you have mastered this information, go on to sheet 6–4.

Name _____

Date _____

Test 6–4

ALMANAC: INTRODUCTION: TEST FRAME

DIRECTIONS: Answer the following questions. As this is a test frame, no answers are given.

1. An almanac is a book containing information about _____,

   _____, and _____.

2. An almanac is published _____.

3. An almanac provides _____ up-to-date information.

4. A well-known almanac is _____.

5. This almanac is better known as _____.

6. This well-known almanac is published _____.

7. This well-known almanac is published in the month of _____.

8. This well-known almanac contains more than one _____

   facts and figures.

9. The index to this well-known almanac is located in the _____

   of the book.

10. The index to this well-known almanac is listed in _____

    order.

Hand in this test to be graded. When you have successfully passed this test, go on to sheet 6–5.

Name _____

Date _____

ALMANAC: USING THE INDEX

Locate the latest edition of *The World Almanac* or use the one assigned to you.

To locate information in *The World Almanac* it is absolutely necessary to use the index.

Locate the index. The index is listed alphabetically by topics (also called headings). Under the topics are subtopics (also called subheadings).

The topics are printed in dark type. Locate the topics.

The subtopics are printed in lighter type and are indented to the second letter. Locate the subtopics.

After locating the topic, if there are subtopics listed, always check the list to zero in on the information.

If the topic you need is not listed, think of synonyms for the topic and check the synonyms.

The most difficult part of using the almanac is trying to determine under what topic the information is listed.

DIRECTIONS:　Cover the answers with your marker. Answer the following questions. Uncover the answers and check your work. Correct if necessary.

1. The index to *The World Almanac* is listed by _____ topics

   and _____. subtopics

2. The topics are listed in _____ type. dark

3. The subtopics are _____ indented

   to the second letter.

When you feel you have mastered this information, go on to sheet 6–6.

Name _____

Date _____

ALMANAC: PRACTICE WITH *THE WORLD ALMANAC*

DIRECTIONS: Locate the latest edition of *The World Almanac* or use the one
assigned to you. Complete the following activities.

1. Edition of *The World Almanac.* _____.

2. Locate the title page. Locate the following:

    Publisher _____. Copyright date _____.

    Editor _____.

3. Locate HIGHLIGHTS at the top of the next page. This section offers an index for
    information concerning the copyright or preceding year. For example, if you are
    using the 1988 edition, the index concerns 1987.

    Locate the listing for: Heroes of Young America. Page _____.

    Who was the "Top Hero" of Young America in the _____ annual
    polling of students in grades 8 - 12?

    Answer _____.

4. Locate HIGHLIGHTS again. Locate the Quick Reference Index. Page _____.
    Locate the page.

    This section offers a shorter index on topics judged most often researched.
    Checking the Quick Reference Index before checking the general index can often be
    a time-saving process.

    a. Checking the Quick Reference Index, on what page will you locate the area
        codes for telephone numbers in all 50 states?

        Page _____.

    b. Locate the page. What other information is included along with the area
        codes? _____.

Hand in this sheet to be checked. When you have successfully completed this page, go on to
sheet 6–7.

Name _____

Date _____

ALMANAC: PRACTICE USING *THE WORLD ALMANAC*

DIRECTIONS: Locate the latest edition of *The World Almanac* or use the one assigned to you. Complete the following activities.

1. Where and when did the first theater open in the American Colonies?

   Page _____   Answer _____

2. Where is Acadia National Park located?

   Page _____   Answer _____

3. What state has the largest number of Indian Reservations?

   Page _____   State _____   Number _____

4. What is the purpose of the Welland Canal?

   Page _____   Answer _____

5. What and when is Forefather's Day?

   Page _____   Answer _____

6. In what mine disaster were the largest number of lives lost?

   Page _____   Date _____   Location _____   Lives Lost _____

7. What is the only surviving Wonder of the Seven Wonders of the World?

   Page _____   Answer _____

8. Where and when was the first commercially productive oil well drilled?

   Page _____   Answer _____

9. According to your almanac, what is the busiest airport in the U.S.A.?

   Page _____   Answer _____

Turn in this sheet to be checked. When you have successfully completed this activity, you have completed the *Almanac* Unit.

UNIT 7

Atlas

Name _____

Date _____

UNIT 7: ATLAS
CHECK-OFF SHEET

DIRECTIONS: Below you will find the names of each activity sheet in UNIT 7. Check off each sheet as it is completed.

INTRODUCTION 7–1	
TYPES OF MAPS 7–2	
REVIEW PAGE 7–3	
TEST FRAME 7–4	
TABLE OF CONTENTS 7–5	
TABLE OF CONTENTS—ACTIVITY PAGE 7–6	
INDEX 7–7	
COPYRIGHT DATE 7–8	
TABLE OF CONTENTS AND INDEX—REVIEW PAGE 7–9	
HEMISPHERES 7–10	
LATITUDE AND LONGITUDE—I 7–11	
LATITUDE AND LONGITUDE—II 7–12	
LATITUDE AND LONGITUDE—ACTIVITY PAGE 7–13	
LATITUDE AND LONGITUDE—REVIEW PAGE 7–14	
HEMISPHERES, LATITUDE, AND LONGITUDE TEST FRAME 7–15	
GRID SQUARES 7–16	
GRID SQUARES—ACTIVITY PAGE 7–17	
SYMBOLS 7–18	
SYMBOLS—ACTIVITY PAGE 7–19	
GRID SQUARES AND SYMBOLS—REVIEW PAGE 7–20	
GRID SQUARES AND SYMBOLS—TEST FRAME 7–21	
FINAL TEST FRAME 7–22	

Name _____

Date _____

ATLAS: INTRODUCTION

An ATLAS is a book or collection of maps, charts, pictures, and other geographical information.

There are two main types of ATLASES.

1. *Geographical atlas.* Provides up-to-date information about the world or parts of the world.

2. *Historical atlas.* Provides information about the world or parts of the world in times past.

In addition to maps, ATLASES provide information such as:

Air, sea, and land distances   Rainfall
Explorations   Temperature
Minerals   Time zones
Population   Universe
Products   Vegetation

DIRECTIONS: Cover the answers with your marker. Answer the following questions. Uncover the answers and check your work. Correct if necessary.

1. A book or collection of maps, charts, pictures, and other

   geographical information is called an _____.   atlas

2. The two main types of atlases are:

   _____ and   geographical

   _____.   historical

When you feel you have mastered this information, go on to sheet 7–2.

Name _____

Date _____

Atlas of
The World

ATLAS: TYPES OF MAPS

There are three main types of maps:

1. Physical maps
2. Political maps
3. Economic maps

A PHYSICAL map, also called a relief map, shows the natural features of the land such as rivers, lakes, mountains, oceans, and deserts.

A POLITICAL map shows the manmade boundaries between places such as countries, states, cities, and towns.

An ECONOMIC map gives information concerning products, population, rainfall, and temperatures.

DIRECTIONS: Cover the answers with your marker. Answer the following questions. Uncover the answers and check your work. Correct if necessary.

1. A map showing the natural features of the land is called a

   _____ map or a   physical

   _____ map.   relief

2. A map showing the manmade boundaries of a country, state, city,

   or town is called a _____ map.   political

3. A map containing information concerning products, population,

   rainfall, and temperature is called an _____   economic

   map.

When you feel you have mastered this information, go on to sheet 7–3.

Name _____

Date _____

ATLAS: REVIEW PAGE

DIRECTIONS: Cover the answers with your marker. Answer the following questions. Uncover the answers and check your work. Correct if necessary.

1. A book or collection of maps, charts, pictures, and other

    geographical information is called an _____.   atlas

2. The two types of atlases are:

    _____ and   geographical

    _____.   historical

3. The three main types of maps are:

    _____,   physical

    _____, and   political

    _____.   economic

4. A map showing the natural features of the land is a

    _____ map.   physical

5. A map showing the manmade boundaries of countries, states, cities,

    or towns is a _____ map.   political

6. A map showing products, population, rainfall, and temperature is

    an _____ map.   economic

When you feel you have mastered this information, go on to sheet 7–4.

© 1990 by The Center for Applied Research in Education

Name _____

Date _____

ATLAS: INTRODUCTION: TEST FRAME

DIRECTIONS: Answer the following questions. As this is a test frame, no answers are given.

1. An atlas is a book of _____ and other information.

2. The two main types of atlases are:

   _____

   _____

3. The three main kinds of maps are:

   _____

   _____

   _____

4. If you wished to know what states of the United States form a boundary with

   Canada, you would use a _____ map.

5. If you wished to know where the Rocky Mountains begin in the north and end in

   the south, you would use a _____ map.

6. If you wished to know the boundaries of the original 13 American Colonies, you

   would use a _____ atlas.

7. If you needed information on what minerals were found in Montana, you would use

   an _____ map.

8. A map of Disneyland would be a _____ map.

9. A map showing the ocean floor would be a _____ map.

Turn in this sheet to be corrected. When you have successfully passed this test, go on to sheet 7–5.

Name _____

Date _____

ATLAS: TABLE OF CONTENTS

The TABLE OF CONTENTS lists the major divisions of the atlas, such as:

The World	States
Continents	Provinces
Countries	Other information

Because each atlas is arranged in a different way, always read the TABLE OF CONTENTS first.

DIRECTIONS: Locate two atlases or use the ones assigned to you. Complete the following activities.

1. Title of first atlas _____

    Publisher _____ Copyright date _____

    Title of second atlas _____

    Publisher _____ Copyright date _____

2. Locate the table of contents in each atlas.

    Each atlas has: _____

    _____

    _____

    The differences in the atlases are:

    The first atlas has: _____

    _____

    The second atlas has: _____

    _____

Take this sheet and the atlases to your teacher to be checked. When you have successfully completed this sheet, go on to sheet 7–6.

Atlas of
The World

Activity 7–6

Name _____

Date _____

ATLAS: TABLE OF CONTENTS: ACTIVITY PAGE

DIRECTIONS: Locate an historical atlas or use the one assigned to you. Complete the following.

1. Title of atlas _____

   Publisher _____ Copyright Date _____

2. Locate the table of contents. Read it.

   What period in time does the atlas cover? _____

   What places does the atlas cover? _____

DIRECTIONS: Locate a geographical atlas or use the one assigned to you. Complete the following.

1. Title of atlas _____

   Publisher _____ Copyright Date _____

2. Locate the table of contents. Read it.

   What places does the atlas cover? _____

3. Locate a physical map. Page _____.

   Locate a political map. Page _____.

4. Locate an economic map. Page _____.

5. Locate another political map. Page _____.

6. Locate another physical map. Page _____.

Turn in this sheet with the atlases to be checked. When you have successfully completed this sheet, go on to sheet 7–7.

Name _____

Date _____

Atlas of

The World

ATLAS: INDEX

The INDEX contains a listing for all specific places included in the atlas.

The INDEX is arranged alphabetically.

The INDEX contains the page number and the letter and number for the grid square within which the place is located. This narrows your search to one grid square.

DIRECTIONS: Locate an atlas or use the one assigned to you. Complete the following activities.

1. Title of atlas _____

   Publisher _____ Copyright date _____.

2. Locate the index. The index begins on page _____.

   What is the first listing? _____.

   Page _____ Letter and number _____.

   Using the listing, locate the place. It is located:

   _____.

   What is the last listing? _____.

   Page _____ Letter and number _____.

   Using the listing, locate the place. It is located:

   _____.

3. Using the index, locate Hamilton, Bermuda. Page _____.

   What ocean surrounds Bermuda? _____.

Take this sheet and the atlas to your teacher to be checked. When you have successfully completed this sheet, go on to sheet 7–8.

© 1990 by The Center for Applied Research in Education

Name _____

Date _____

ATLAS: COPYRIGHT DATE

Because our world is always changing due to natural and manmade causes, it is very important to use the latest atlas available.

Old or out-of-date information is not acceptable except for historical purposes.

Most libraries contain a collection of atlases. Always check the copyright date before selecting an atlas.

DIRECTIONS: Locate the atlas collection. Using only the geographical atlases, complete the following activities.

1. Locate the atlas collection. List the titles available.

   A. Title _____

   Publisher _____ Copyright date _____

   B. Title _____

   Publisher _____ Copyright date _____

   C. Title _____

   Publisher _____ Copyright date _____

   D. Title _____

   Publisher _____ Copyright date _____

   E. Title _____

   Publisher _____ Copyright date _____

2. Which is the latest atlas? _____

   Which is the oldest atlas? _____

Using the latest atlas, complete the activities on sheet 7–9.

Name _____

Date _____

ATLAS: TABLE OF CONTENTS AND INDEX: REVIEW PAGE

DIRECTIONS: Locate an atlas or use the one assigned to you. Complete the following activities.

1. Title of atlas _____

    Publisher _____ Copyright date _____

2. Locate the table of contents. Page _____

3. Using the table of contents, locate a political map of the world.

    a. Is the United States located in the northern or southern hemisphere?

    _____

    b. Is Africa located in the eastern or western hemisphere?

    _____

4. Locate the index. Page _____

5. Using the index, locate the listing for Santiago, Chile.

    Page _____ Letter _____ Number _____

    Locate the city.

6. Using the index, locate the listing for Liverpool, England.

    Page _____ Letter _____ Number _____

    Locate the city. What city in Ireland is directly west?

    _____

Take this sheet and the atlas to your teacher. Locate activities 1 - 6 for your teacher. When you have successfully completed this sheet, go on to sheet 7–10.

Name _____

Date _____

ATLAS: HEMISPHERES

The earth's shape is a sphere. Half of a sphere is a hemisphere.

The *top* half of the earth is called the *northern* hemisphere.

The *bottom* half of the earth is called the *southern* hemisphere.

The *left* half of the earth is called the *western* hemisphere.

The *right* half of the earth is called the *eastern* hemisphere.

Maps usually have a compass printed on the page to tell you where north is located.

DIRECTIONS: Cover the answers with your marker. Answer the following questions. Uncover the answers and check your work. Correct if necessary.

1. The earth's shape is a _____.   sphere

2. Half of a sphere is a _____.   hemisphere

3. The top half of the earth is called the _____   northern

    hemisphere.

4. The bottom half of the earth is called the _____   southern

    hemisphere.

5. The left half of the earth is called the _____   western

    hemisphere.

6. The right half of the hemisphere is called the

    _____.   eastern

7. Most maps have a _____ to   compass

    help you locate north.

When you feel you have mastered this information, go on to sheet 7–11.

Name _____

Date _____

ATLAS: LATITUDE AND LONGITUDE—I

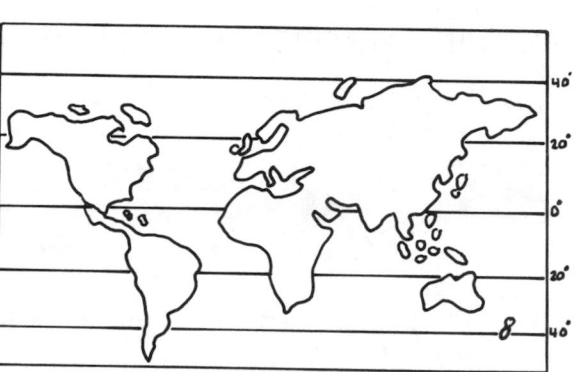

LATITUDE and LONGITUDE are imaginary lines drawn on maps and globes as an aid to locating places on the earth.

LATITUDE lines are also called parallel lines. LATITUDE lines run east-west around the earth.

LATITUDE is measured in degrees, beginning at the equator which is 0 degrees.

Above the equator is north and below the equator is south.

DIRECTIONS: Cover the answers with your marker. Answer the following questions. Uncover the answers and check your work. Correct if necessary.

1. Latitude and longitude are _____   imaginary

   lines drawn on maps and globes.

2. Latitude and longitude lines are an aide in _____   locating

   places on the earth.

3. Latitude lines are also called _____ lines.   parallel

4. Latitude lines run _____ around the earth.   east-west

5. Latitude is measured in _____ beginning   degrees

   at the _____.   equator

6. The equator is _____ degrees.   0

7. Above the equator is _____ and below the   north

   equator is _____.   south

When you feel you have mastered this information, go on to sheet 7–12.

Name _____

Date _____

ATLAS: LATITUDE AND LONGITUDE—II

LATITUDE and LONGITUDE are imaginary lines drawn on maps and globes as an aid to locating places on the earth.

LONGITUDE lines are also called meridian lines. LONGITUDE lines run north-south around the earth.

LONGITUDE is measured in degrees from the prime meridian or 0, which is located in Greenwich, England.

To the right of the prime meridian is east and to the left of the prime meridian is west.

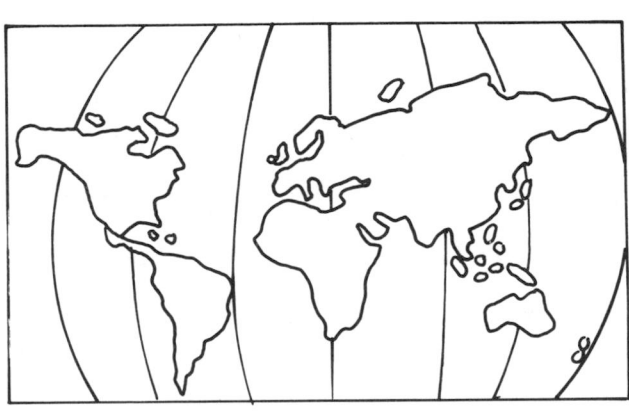

DIRECTIONS: Cover the answers with your marker. Answer the following questions. Uncover the answers and check your work. Correct if necessary.

1. Latitude and longitude are _____ lines   imaginary

   drawn on maps and globes.

2. Longitude lines are also called _____   meridian

   lines.

3. Longitude lines run _____   north-south

   around the earth.

4. Longitude is measured in degrees from the

   _____ located   prime meridian

   in Greenwich, _____.   England

5. To the right of the prime meridian is _____, and   east

   to the left of the prime meridian is _____.   west

When you feel you have mastered this information, go on to sheet 7–13.

Name _____

Date _____

ATLAS: LATITUDE AND LONGITUDE: ACTIVITY PAGE

DIRECTIONS: Locate an atlas or use the one assigned to you. Complete the following activities.

1. Title of atlas _____

    Publisher _____ Copyright Date _____.

2. Using the table of contents, locate a map of the world.

    Page _____.

3. Locate the following:

    a. Latitude or parallel lines.

    b. The equator and 0 degrees latitude.

4. Latitude or parallel lines run in the direction of:

    _____.

5. Locate the following:

    a. Longitude or meridian lines.

    b. Prime meridian and 0 degrees.

6. Longitude or meridian lines run in the direction of:

    _____.

7. Locate the following:

    a. The northern hemisphere—the southern hemisphere.

    b. The eastern hemisphere—the western hemisphere.

Take the atlas and this sheet to your teacher. Locate activities 1 - 7 for your teacher. When you have successfully completed this sheet, go on to sheet 7–14.

Name _____

Date _____

ATLAS: LATITUDE AND LONGITUDE: REVIEW PAGE

DIRECTIONS: Cover the answers with your marker. Answer the following questions. Uncover the answers and check your work. Correct if necessary.

1. _____ and _____ are   Latitude
                                                                     longitude
   imaginary lines drawn on maps and globes.

2. Latitude lines are also called _____   parallel

   lines.

3. Latitude lines run _____   east-west

   around the earth.

4. Latitude is measured in degrees beginning at the

   _____ .   equator

5. Above the equator is _____ and below   north

   the equator is _____ .   south

6. Longitude lines are also called _____ lines.   meridian

7. Longitude lines run _____   north-south

   around the earth.

8. Longitude is measured in degrees from the _____   prime

   meridian located in Greenwich, _____ .   England

9. To the right of the prime meridian is _____ and   east

   to the left of the prime meridian is _____ .   west

When you feel you have mastered this information, go on to sheet 7–15.

Name _____

Date _____

ATLAS: HEMISPHERES, LATITUDE, AND LONGITUDE: TEST FRAME

© 1990 by The Center for Applied Research in Education

DIRECTIONS: Answer the following questions. As this is a test frame, no answers are given.

1. The earth's shape is a _____.

2. One-half of the earth's shape is a _____.

3. The top half of the earth is called the _____.

4. The lower half of the earth is called the _____.

5. The left half of the earth is called the _____.

6. The right half of the earth is called the _____.

7. Maps usually show a _____ to tell where north is located.

8. Imaginary parallel lines running east-west around the earth are known as

_____.

9. These parallel lines are measured in degrees beginning at the _____

which is _____ degrees.

10. Imaginary meridian lines running north-south from the poles are known as

_____.

11. These meridian lines are measured in degrees from Greenwich, England which is

called the _____ meridian and is _____ degrees.

12. The parallel and meridian lines are used as an aid to help _____

places on the earth.

Turn in this test to be corrected. When you pass the test, go on to sheet 7–16.

Name _____

Date _____

ATLAS: GRID SQUARES

Intersecting latitude lines and longitude lines form GRID SQUARES which help in locating places on the map.

The GRID SQUARES are formed by the intersecting lines.

Letters, and sometimes numbers, are used to identify the GRID SQUARES.

The letters, and sometimes numbers, are printed across the top and bottom and along the sides of the map.

When given the letter and number of the place to be located, the search is narrowed to one GRID SQUARE.

DIRECTIONS: Cover the answers with your marker. Answer the following questions. Uncover the answers and check your work. Correct if necessary.

1. Latitude and longitude lines form _____   grid

   squares.

2. These squares are formed by the lines

   _____.   intersecting

3. These squares are identified by _____   letters

   and sometimes numbers.

4. The letters and numbers are printed on the _____   top

   and bottom and along the _____ of the map.   sides

5. Given the letter and number, the search is narrowed to

   _____ grid.   one

When you feel you have mastered this information, go on to sheet 7–17.

Name _____

Date _____

ATLAS: GRID SQUARES: ACTIVITY PAGE

DIRECTIONS: Locate an atlas or use the one assigned to you. Complete the
following activities.

1. Title of atlas _____

    Publisher _____ Copyright date _____.

2. Locate a map of North America. Page _____.

3. Locate the equator. Locate the latitude or parallel lines.

    How many degrees are there between lines? _____ degrees.

4. Locate the prime meridian. Locate the longitude or meridian lines. How many

    degrees are there between line? _____ degrees.

5. Look at the top and bottom of the map. What letters or numbers are used?

    _____.

6. Look along the sides of the map. What letters or numbers are used?

    _____.

7. Locate the grid squares.

8. Follow a number or letter at the top or bottom of the map and a number or letter

    along the side of the map until they intersect.

    Number or letter at top _____ Number or letter along the side _____.

    Follow the two until they intersect.

9. Locate a place within the grid square at the intersection.

    Place _____.

Take the atlas and this sheet to your teacher. Locate activities 1 - 9 for your teacher. When
you have successfully completed this sheet, go on to sheet 7–18.

Name _____

Date _____

ATLAS: SYMBOLS

A SYMBOL represents or stands for something. Maps use SYMBOLS to include a variety of information in a small space.

Each atlas or map has a LEGEND, which may also be called a code, which is the key to the SYMBOLS used.

The LEGEND is usually printed in a small box at a corner of each map.

The LEGEND may show:

    A. The capital of a country or state.
    B. A scale of miles or kilometers to the inch.
    C. Symbolic figures or picture language.
    D. Altitude—usually shown by color.
    E. Roads, railroads, or shipping lanes.

DIRECTIONS: Cover the answers with your marker. Answer the following questions. Uncover the answers and check your work. Correct if necessary.

1. Each atlas or map has a _____ or   legend

   code that is the key to the information found on a map.

2. This code is usually printed in a small box at a

   _____ of the map.   corner

3. The legend may show: _____,   capital
                                         scale of miles
  _____, _____,   symbolic figures
                                          altitude
  _____, _____   roads

  _____.   shipping lanes

When you feel you have mastered this information, go on to sheet 7–19.

Name _____

Date _____

Atlas of
The World

ATLAS: SYMBOLS: ACTIVITY PAGE

DIRECTIONS: Locate an atlas or use the one assigned to you. Complete the following activities.

1. Title of atlas _____

   Publisher _____ Copyright date _____ .

2. Locate a physical map of the United States or Canada. Page _____ .

   Locate the legend. What information does the legend show?

   _____

   _____

   _____

   _____

3. Locate a political map of the United States or Canada. Page _____ .

   Locate the legend. What information does the legend show?

   _____

   _____

   _____

   _____

4. Locate an economic map of the United States or Canada. Page _____ .

   Locate the legend. What information does the legend show?

   _____

   _____

Take this sheet and the atlas to your teacher to be checked. When you have successfully completed this activity, go on to sheet 7–20.

Name _____

Date _____

Atlas of
The World

ATLAS: GRID SQUARES AND SYMBOLS:
REVIEW PAGE

DIRECTIONS: Cover the answers with your marker. Answer the following questions. Uncover the answers and check your work. Correct if necessary.

1. Latitude and longitude lines form _____   grid

   squares.

2. These squares are formed by the lines

   _____.   intersecting

3. These squares are identified by _____   letters

   and sometimes numbers.

4. These letters and numbers are printed along the _____   top

   and bottom and along the _____ of the map.   sides

5. When you know the letter and number, the search is narrowed to

   _____ grid square.   one

6. Each atlas or map has a code or _____.   legend

   That is the key to the information found on the map.

7. The code is usually printed in a small box at a

   _____ of the map.   corner

8. One type of information the legend always shows is the

   _____ of miles or kilometers.   scale

When you feel you have mastered this information, go on to sheet 7–21.

Name _____

Date _____

ATLAS: GRID SQUARES AND SYMBOLS: TEST FRAME

© 1990 by The Center for Applied Research in Education

DIRECTIONS: Answer the following questions. As this is a test frame, no answers are given.

1. Grid squares are formed by the _____ or parallel lines and the _____ or meridian lines.

2. Grid squares are formed by the lines _____.

3. Grid squares are identified by _____ and sometimes numbers.

4. These _____ and numbers are found on the _____ and bottom and along the _____ of the map.

5. Using the _____ and numbers helps you to narrow your search for a place to _____ grid square.

6. Each atlas has a code or _____ to explain the information found on the map.

7. The code or information is usually printed in a small box at a _____ of the map.

8. Name several types of information that may be included in the code.

   _____

   _____

   _____

   _____

Turn in this test to be corrected. When you have successfully passed the test, go on to sheet 7–22.

Atlas of

The World

Name _____

Date _____

ATLAS: FINAL TEST FRAME

DIRECTIONS: Using an atlas, locate the answers to the following questions. As this is a test frame, no answers are given.

1. Is New Zealand located in the northern or southern hemisphere?

   _____

2. Is Saudi Arabia located in the eastern or western hemisphere?

   _____

3. On which Japanese Island is the city of Sapporo located?

   _____

4. What sea separates Ireland and England?

   _____

5. What is the capital city of Switzerland?

   _____

6. What country is directly north of the country of Sudan?

   _____

7. Alaska shares a border with which Canadian territory?

   _____

8. Lima, Peru is located on the coast of what ocean?

   _____

9. What island is located off the toe of Italy?

   _____

Turn in this test to be corrected. When you have successfully passed this test, you have completed the *Atlas* Unit.

UNIT 8

The Readers' Guide to Periodical Literature

Name _____

Date _____

UNIT 8: THE *READERS' GUIDE TO PERIODICAL LITERATURE* CHECK-OFF SHEET

DIRECTIONS: Below you will find the names of each activity in UNIT 8. Check off each sheet as it is completed.

THE *READERS' GUIDE:* INTRODUCTION 8–1	
INFORMATION 8–2	
REVIEW PAGE 8–3	
TEST FRAME 8–4	
ABBREVIATIONS 8–5	
ABBREVIATIONS ACTIVITY 8–6	
DECODING AN ENTRY 8–7	
ACTIVITY PAGE—I 8–8	
ACTIVITY PAGE—II 8–9	
TEST FRAME—I 8–10	
TEST FRAME—II 8–11	

Name _____

Date _____

THE *READERS' GUIDE TO PERIODICAL LITERATURE*: INTRODUCTION

A PERIODICAL is a magazine published weekly, biweekly, monthly, or at longer intervals throughout the year.

There are hundreds of periodicals or magazines published each year, containing thousands of articles.

The *Readers' Guide to Periodical Literature* is an index to the articles published in most magazines each year.

The *Readers' Guide to Periodical Literature* is indexed by author and subject.

The *Readers' Guide to Periodical Literature* also indexes media reviews.

The *Readers' Guide to Periodical Literature* is a reference tool to assist in locating information quickly.

The *Readers' Guide to Periodical Literature* is most commonly known as the *Readers' Guide*.

DIRECTIONS: Cover the answers with your marker. Answer the following questions. Uncover the answers and check your work. Correct if necessary.

1. A periodical is a _____.   magazine

2. The *Readers' Guide* is an _____.   index

3. The *Readers' Guide* is indexed by _____   author

   and _____.   subject

4. The *Readers' Guide* also contains an index to

   _____ reviews.   media

When you feel you have mastered this information, go on to sheet 8–2.

Name _____

Date _____

THE *READERS' GUIDE:* INFORMATION

The *Readers' Guide* is published:

1. Monthly or bimonthly
2. Quarterly
3. Yearly

The *Readers' Guide* contains the following information.

1. The subject of the article.
2. The author and title of the article.
3. The title of the magazine.
4. The volume and/or issue number.
5. The page numbers of the article.
6. The date the magazine was published.

The *Readers' Guide* is cross-referenced to help in locating information.

DIRECTIONS: Cover the answers with your marker. Answer the following questions. Uncover the answers and check your work. Correct if necessary.

1. The *Readers' Guide* contains the following information:

   a. The _____ of the article.   subject

   b. The _____ and   author

   _____ of the article.   title

   c. The _____ of the magazine.   title

   d. The _____ and/or   volume

   _____ number of the magazine.   issue

   e. The _____ numbers of the article.   page

   f. The _____ the magazine was published.   date

When you feel you have mastered this information, go on to sheet 8–3.

Name _____

Date _____

THE *READERS' GUIDE*: REVIEW PAGE

DIRECTIONS: Cover the answers with your marker. Answer the following questions. Uncover the answers and check your work. Correct if necessary.

1. A periodical is a _____.   magazine

2. The *Readers' Guide* is an _____ to   index

   articles published in magazines.

3. The *Readers' Guide* is published _____ or   monthly
   or
   bi-monthly
   _____, _____,   quarterly

   and _____.   yearly

4. The *six* items of information found in each entry of the

   Readers' Guide are:

   1. _____   subject

   2. _____   author

   3. _____   title

   4. _____   volume or
   issue number
   5. _____   page number
   date of
   6. _____   magazine

5. The *Readers' Guide* also contains an index to

   _____ reviews.   media

6. The *Readers' Guide* is a reference tool to assist in locating

   _____ quickly.   information

When you feel you have mastered this information, go on to sheet 8–4.

Name _____

Date _____

THE *READERS' GUIDE*: TEST FRAME

DIRECTIONS: Answer the following questions. As this is a test frame, no answers are given.

1. A periodical is a _____ .

2. The *Readers' Guide* is an _____ to articles published in periodicals.

3. The *Readers Guide* is indexed by _____ and by

   _____ .

4. The *Readers' Guide* also contains an index to _____ reviews.

5. The *Readers' Guide* is a reference tool to assist in locating _____

   quickly.

6. Name 6 items of information found in each entry in the *Readers' Guide*.

   _____

   _____

   _____

   _____

   _____

   _____

7. The *Readers' Guide* is published:

   _____

   _____

   _____

Turn in this test to be graded. When you pass the test, go on to sheet 8–5.

Name _____

Date _____

THE *READERS' GUIDE*
ABBREVIATIONS IN THE *READERS' GUIDE*

The *Readers' Guide* makes use of ABBREVIATIONS. The ABBREVIATIONS INDEX is found in the front of each issue.

It is necessary to know what each ABBREVIATION stands for in order to decode each entry.

DIRECTIONS: Cover the answers with your marker. Complete the following activities. Uncover the answers and check your work. Correct if necessary.

DIRECTIONS: Locate an issue of the *Readers' Guide* or use the one assigned to you. Write the full meaning of the abbreviations found below.

EXAMPLE: ann   __annual__

1. Aut   _____   Autumn

2. bldg   _____   building

3. Jl   _____   July

4. q   _____   quarterly

5. v   _____   volume

6. sec   _____   section

7. por   _____   portrait

8. rev   _____   revised

9. O   _____   October

10. Sr   _____   Senior

When you feel you have mastered this information, go on to sheet 8–6.

Name _____

Date _____

THE *READERS' GUIDE*
ABBREVIATIONS ACTIVITY PAGE

DIRECTIONS: Locate an issue of the *Readers' Guide* or use the one assigned to you. Locate the index to abbreviations. Write the full meaning of the abbreviations found below.

1. bi-w _____   16. yr _____

2. Co _____   17. Inc _____

3. Je _____   18. Soc _____

4. m _____   19. abr _____

5. Sq _____   20. il _____

6. bibl _____   21. bi-m _____

7. + _____   22. cont _____

8. Mr _____   23. Ltd _____

9. Spr _____   24. Sp _____

10. Corp _____   25. pub _____

11. Ja _____   26. Summ _____

12. Dept _____   27. ed _____

13. supp _____   28. tr _____

14. My _____   29. w _____

15. pt _____   30. supt _____

Turn in this sheet and the issue of the *Readers' Guide* to be checked. When you have successfully completed this activity, go on to sheet 8–7.

Name _____

Date _____

THE *READERS' GUIDE*: DECODING AN ENTRY

Each entry in the *Readers' Guide* is arranged in the same order.

When you understand the order, DECODING AN ENTRY becomes easy.
EXAMPLE: An entry in the *Readers' Guide* is organized in the following order.

1. SUBJECT OR AUTHOR HEADING (IN CAPITAL LETTERS)
2. Title of the article
3. Author of the article (if subject heading is used)
4. Abbreviations where applicable
5. Title of the magazine (printed in italics)
6. Issue or volume number (followed by a colon)
7. Page number or numbers (following the colon)
8. Date of issue of the magazine

An entry in the *Readers' Guide* would be decoded as follows:

> MOTORCYCLE OWNERSHIP
> My motorcycle years. J. H. Kunstler. il *Gentleman's Quarterly* 58: 93+ Ap '88

1. MOTORCYCLE OWNERSHIP . . . SUBJECT HEADING
2. My motorcycle years . . . . Title of the article
3. J.H. Kunstler . . . . Author of the article
4. il . . . . Article has illustrations
5. *Gentleman's Quarterly* . . . . Title of the magazine
6. 58: . . . . Volume number of the magazine
7. 93 . . . . Page the article begins on
8. + ... Article continued on later pages
9. Ap '88 . . . . Date of magazine - April 1988

When you feel you have mastered this information, go on to sheet 8–8.

Name _____

Date _____

THE *READERS' GUIDE*: DECODING AN ENTRY: ACTIVITY PAGE—I

DIRECTIONS: Using the sheet, DECODING AN ENTRY, decode the following sample entry from the *Readers' Guide.*

ROCK & ROLL HALL OF FAME
    Rock & Roll Hall of Fame dinner. J. Levenson. il *Down Beat* 55:11 Ap '88

Subject heading _____

Title of article _____

Author _____

il _____

Title of magazine _____

Volume number _____

Page or pages _____

Date of magazine _____

Turn in this sheet to be checked. When you have successfully completed this sheet, go on to sheet 8–9.

Name _____

Date _____

**THE *READERS' GUIDE*: DECODING AN
ENTRY: ACTIVITY PAGE—II**

DIRECTIONS: Using the sheet, DECODING AN ENTRY, decode the following
sample entry from the *Readers' Guide.*

> ROONEY, ANDREW A.
>   Hip, hip, but no hooray. il *The Saturday Evening Post*
>   260:14 Ap '88

Subject heading _____

Title of article _____

Author _____

il _____

Title of magazine _____

Volume number _____

Page or pages _____

Date of magazine _____

Turn in this sheet to be checked. When you have successfully completed this sheet, go on to
sheet 8–10.

Name _____

Date _____

THE *READERS' GUIDE*: TEST FRAME—I

DIRECTIONS: Decode the following entries from the *Reader's Guide.*

1.

> MOUNT EVEREST (CHINA AND NEPAL)
> The adventures of National Geographic [expedition]
> il maps *National Geographic World* 152:12–15 Ap '88

_____

_____

_____

_____

_____

_____

_____

_____

_____

_____

_____

© 1990 by The Center for Applied Research in Education

Go on to sheet 8–11.

Name _____

Date _____

THE *READERS' GUIDE*: TEST FRAME—I

DIRECTIONS: Decode the following entry from the *Readers' Guide.*

1.

> ROSS, STEVEN S.
>   Software review for architects. il *Architectural
>   Record* 176:125+ Ap '88

_____

_____

_____

_____

_____

_____

_____

_____

_____

_____

Turn in this test to be graded. When you pass the test, you have completed the *Readers' Guide* Unit.

UNIT 9

Famous
First Facts

Name _____

Date _____

UNIT 9: *FAMOUS FIRST FACTS*
CHECK-OFF SHEET

DIRECTIONS: Below you will find the names of each activity in UNIT 9. Check off each
sheet as it is completed.

FAMOUS FIRST FACTS 9–1	
INDEX—SUBJECT INDEX 9–2	
INDEX BY YEARS 9–3	
INDEX BY DAYS OF THE MONTH 9–4	
INDEX TO PERSONAL NAMES 9–5	
INDEX BY GEOGRAPHICAL LOCATION 9–6	
REVIEW PAGE 9–7	
TEST FRAME 9–8	

Name _____

Date _____

KANE, JOSEPH NATHAN. *FAMOUS FIRST FACTS*

FAMOUS FIRST FACTS is a reference book. The fourth edition of *Famous First Facts* contains more than 9,000 "firsts" from the year 1007 through 1981.

Famous First Facts is a book of: who, what, when, and where.

Famous First Facts reports the first discoveries, happenings, and inventions occurring throughout the history of America.

DIRECTIONS: Cover the answers with your marker. Answer the following questions. Uncover the answers and check your work. Correct if necessary.

1. The author of *Famous First Facts* is

   _____ .

   Kane, Joseph Nathan

2. *Famous First Facts* contains more than _____

   "firsts."

   9,000

3. *Famous First Facts* is a book of:

   _____   _____

   who, what

   _____   _____

   when, where

4. *Famous First Facts* covers the years

   _____ to _____ .

   1007, 1981

5. *Famous First Facts* contains the "firsts" throughout

   _____ history.

   American

When you feel you have mastered this information, go on to sheet 9–2.

Name _____

Date _____

FAMOUS FIRST FACTS: INDEX

Famous First Facts has five separate indexes to assist in locating information.

Famous First Facts is indexed by:

Subject   Personal names
Year   Geographic location
Month and day

Subject index

The facts in the subject index are listed alphabetically by subject and use cross-references.

The main subjects or headings are printed in capital letters.
The subheadings are printed in dark or boldface type.

DIRECTIONS: Locate a copy of *Famous First Facts* or use the one assigned to you. Cover the answers with your marker. Answer the following questions. Uncover the answers and check your work. Correct if necessary.

1. Turn to the contents page. The section Famous First Facts

   begins on page _____.   1

2. Turn to that page. How is this section arranged?

   _____.   alphabetically

3. The main subjects or headings are printed in

   _____ letters.   capital

4. The subheadings are printed in _____ or   dark

   _____ type.   boldface

5. The index ends on page _____.   718

When you feel you have mastered this information, go on to sheet 9–3.

Name _____

Date _____

FAMOUS FIRST FACTS

Famous First Facts is indexed by:

Subject

Year

Index by Years

The year, arranged from the earliest to the latest date, is the main heading. The first facts for each year are listed alphabetically.

The dark or boldface type gives the subject under which more information can be found in the subject index.

DIRECTIONS: Locate a copy of *Famous First Facts* or use the one assigned to you. Cover the answers with your marker. Answer the following questions. Uncover the answers and check your work. Correct if necessary.

1. Locate the contents page. The section Index by Years begins

   on page _____.   719

2. Turn to that page. The index begins with the year _____.   1007

3. The first for each year are listed in

   _____ order.   alphabetical

4. The dark or boldface type shows that more information may

   be found in the _____ index.   subject

5. What first occurred in 1689?

   _____.   newspaper, schoolbook

When you feel you have mastered this information, go on to sheet 9–4.

Name _____

Date _____

FAMOUS FIRST FACTS

Famous First Facts is indexed by:

    Subject

    Year

    Month and day

Index by Days of the Month

    The month and day is the main heading. The facts are listed in numerical order.

    The dark or boldface type gives the subject under which information may be found in the subject index.

DIRECTIONS: Locate a copy of *Famous First Facts* or use the one assigned to you. Cover the answers with your marker. Answer the following questions. Uncover the answers and check your work. Correct if necessary.

1. Locate the contents page. The section Index by Days of the

   Month begins on page _____.   893

2. Turn to that page. The index begins with the date

   _____.   January 1

3. The month and day is the main heading. The facts are listed

   in _____ order.   numerical

4. What first occurred on February 6, 1956?

   _____   first circular

   _____   school built;
                                      Kankakee, Ill.

When you feel you have mastered this information, go on to sheet 9–5.

Name _____

Date _____

FAMOUS FIRST FACTS

Famous First Facts is indexed by:

Subject   Personal names

Year

Month and day

Index to Personal Names

Personal names are listed in alphabetical order.
The dark or boldface type gives the subject under which more information may be found in the subject index.

DIRECTIONS: Locate a copy of *Famous First Facts* or use the one assigned to you. Cover the answers with your marker. Answer the following questions. Uncover the answers and check your work. Correct if necessary.

1. Locate the contents page. The section Index to Personal

   Names begins on page _____.   893

2. Turn to that page. The first name listed in the index is

   _____.   Hank Aaron

3. The dark or boldface type shows that more information may be

   found in the subject index under _____   Baseball

   _____.   Team

4. Look up Heco, Joseph. Who was Joseph Heco?

   Joseph Heco was the first _____   Japanese

   _____   granted
                                    citizenship
   When? _____   Where? _____   June 30, 1858
                                                          Baltimore, Md.

When you feel you have mastered this information, go on to sheet 9–6.

Name _____

Date _____

FAMOUS FIRST FACTS

Famous First Facts is indexed by:

Subject   Personal names

Year   Geographic location

Month and day

Geographical index

The states, listed alphabetically, are the main headings. Cities and towns are listed alphabetically under each state.

The facts are listed alphabetically under each city or town. The dark or boldface type gives the subject under which more information may be found in the subject index.

DIRECTIONS: Locate a copy of *Famous First Facts* or use the one assigned to you. Cover the answers with your marker. Answer the following questions. Uncover the answers and check your work. Correct if necessary.

1. Locate the contents page. The section Geographical Index

    begins on page _____.   1199

2. Turn to that page. The first subject listed under *Alabama*

    is _____.   Boycott Law

3. If you need more information on Boycott Law, you would look

    under _____   Boycott Law

    in the subject index.

4. Look up, Galva, Illinois. The first two women postal clerks

    were _____   Maude Olson

    and _____.   Mary Olson

When you feel you have mastered this information, go on to sheet 9–7.

Name _____

Date _____

1ST:
- who
- what
- where
- when

Famous First Facts

FAMOUS FIRST FACTS: REVIEW PAGE

DIRECTIONS: Cover the answers with your marker. Answer the following questions. Uncover the answers and check your work. Correct if necessary.

1. *Famous First Facts* is a _____ book.   reference

2. *Famous First Facts* is a book of _____, _____,   who, what

   _____, and _____.   when, where

3. *Famous First Facts* covers the firsts throughout the history of

   _____.   America

4. *Famous First Facts* contains five different indexes.

   1. Index by _____.   subject

   2. Index by _____.   year

   3. Index by _____.   month and day

   4. Index by _____.   personal names

   5. Index by _____.   geographic location

5. The dark or boldface type gives the _____   subject

   under which more information may be found in the

   _____ index.   subject

6. The listings give the _____   first time

   for each occurrence.

When you feel you have mastered this information, go on to sheet 9-8.

Name _____

Date _____

FAMOUS FIRST FACTS: TEST FRAME

1ST:
- who
- what
- where
- when

Famous First Facts

DIRECTIONS: Locate a copy of *Famous First Facts* or use the one assigned to you. Complete the following activities.

1. The first alarm clock was made by _____

    of _____ in _____.

2. The first American encyclopedia was the _____,

    edited by _____. The set contained

    _____, volumes. The final volume was published in the year _____.

3. The first state school for the blind was opened in 1837. It was opened in the city of

    _____ on _____.

4. In 1905, the first theater devoted exclusively to motion pictures opened on

    _____ in _____.

5. On April 25th, in the year _____, the first Japanese Ambassador arrived in

    _____.

6. Melvin C. Garlow was the first pilot to fly a million miles in a jet plane. He flew his

    millionth mile on _____. His first flight was made in

    a _____ in the year _____.

7. In Norwich, Connecticut, the first typewriter that successfully typed was patented

    by _____ on _____.

8. In Mount Desert, Maine, the first national park east of the Mississippi, was

    established on _____ in the year _____.

Turn in this sheet to be checked. When you have successfully completed this sheet, you have completed the *Famous First Facts* Unit.

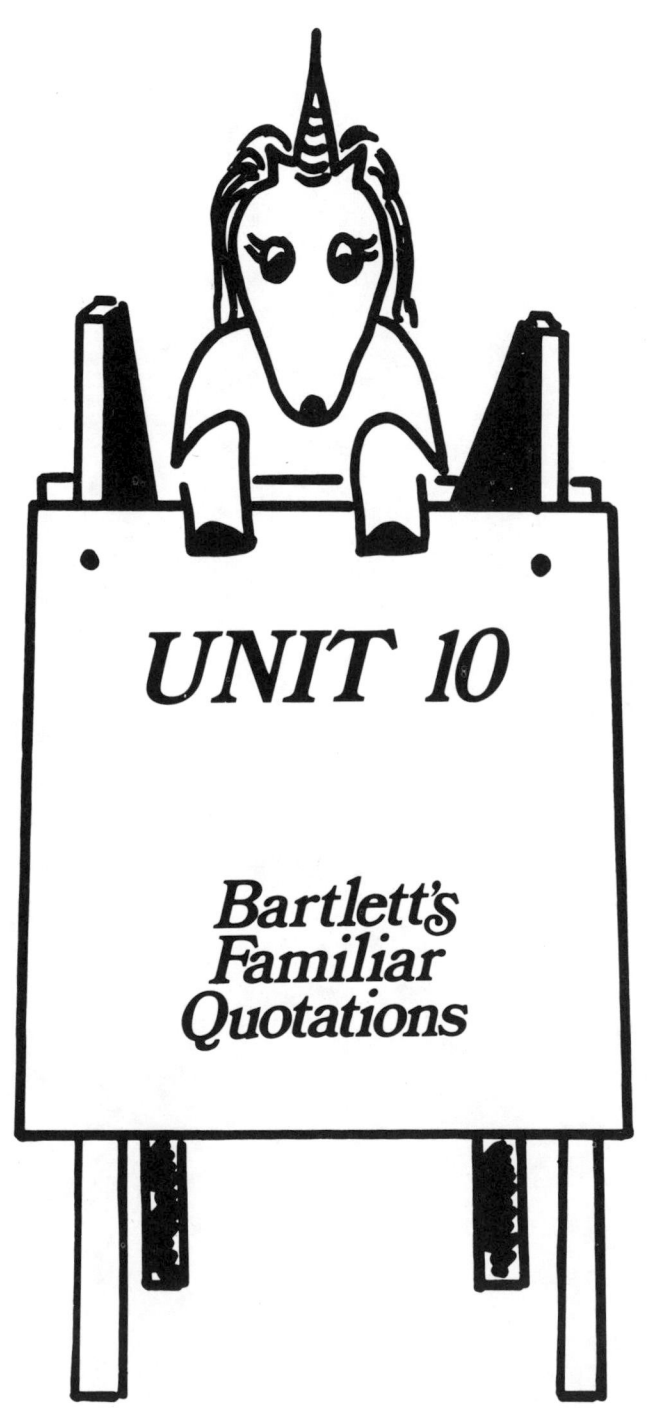

UNIT 10

Bartlett's Familiar Quotations

Name _____

Date _____

UNIT 10: *BARTLETT'S FAMILIAR QUOTATIONS* CHECK-OFF SHEET

DIRECTIONS: Below you will find the names of each activity in UNIT 10. Check off each sheet as it is completed.

BARTLETT'S FAMILIAR QUOTATIONS —INTRODUCTION 10–1	
ACTIVITY PAGE I 10–2	
ACTIVITY PAGE II 10–3	
PRACTICE USING *BARTLETT'S* 10–4	
PRACTICE USING *BARTLETT'S* CONTINUED 10–5	
REVIEW PAGE 10–6	
TEST FRAME 10–7	
PRACTICE ACTIVITIES 10–8	

Name _____

Date _____

BARTLETT'S FAMILIAR QUOTATIONS: INTRODUCTION

BARTLETT'S FAMILIAR QUOTATIONS is a reference book.

Its proper title is:

Familiar Quotations: A Collection of Passages, Phrases, and Proverbs Traced to Their Source.

It is most commonly known as *BARTLETT'S.*

Bartlett's is a collection of famous sayings.

Bartlett's was first originated by John Bartlett in 1855. Today it is edited by a staff at Little, Brown, and Company.

Bartlett's contains more than 22,000 quotations.

DIRECTIONS: Cover the answers with your marker. Answer the following questions. Uncover the answers and check your work. Correct if necessary.

1. *Bartlett's* is a _____ book.

   reference

2. *Bartlett's* is a _____ of

   _____.

   collection
   famous
   sayings

3. *Bartlett's* was first originated by _____

   _____ in _____.

   John
   Bartlett
   1855

4. Today *Bartlett's* is edited by a staff at _____

   _____.

   Little,
   Brown, and
   Company

5. *Bartlett's* contains more than _____

   quotations.

   22,000

When you feel you have mastered this information, go on to sheet 10–2.

Name _____

Date _____

BARTLETT'S FAMILIAR QUOTATIONS: ACTIVITY PAGE I

DIRECTIONS: Locate a copy of *Bartlett's* or use the copy assigned to you. Complete the following activities.

1. What is the latest copyright date? _____.

2. Who is the editor? _____.

3. Turn to the *contents* page. Locate the page number for *The Guide to the Use of Familiar Quotations.* Turn to that page.

   a. Check the heading, *Basic Information.* Notice that the book is arranged by author birth date, from the earliest to the latest authors.

   b. Check the heading, *Author Headings.* Notice that each author heading contains the birth date and death date (where applicable) under the name of the author. Authors with the same birth year are arranged alphabetically. Each author's works are arranged from the earliest works to the latest works.

   c. Check the heading, *Quotations.* Notice the use of *Ib.,* which is the abbreviation of *Ibidem,* which means in the same place. If the source is the same as the source already given, rather than repeat, *Ib.* is used. If a different part of the work is being quoted, that information is given, along with *Ib.* Simply follow *Ib.* back to the source.

4. Locate the *Index of Authors.* Who is the first author given?

   Name _____

   Birth/death date _____ Page _____

5. Using the *Index of Authors,* who is the last author given?

   Name _____

   Birth/death date _____ Page _____

When you feel you have mastered this information, turn in this sheet and the copy of *Bartlett's* to be checked. When you have successfully completed this page, go on to sheet 10–3.

Name _____

Date _____

BARTLETT'S FAMILIAR QUOTATIONS: ACTIVITY PAGE II

DIRECTIONS: Locate a copy of *Bartlett's* or use the one assigned to you. Complete the following activities.

1. Locate the *Contents* page. Locate the *Index*. Turn to the page given.

2. The index is the most important section of *Bartlett's*. *Bartlett's* is most generally used to locate the author, the title, or the whole work, when only a few words of the first line are known.

3. The index is listed alphabetically by one of the words in the first phrase, line, or sentence. *Please note* that the first word is not always used. If the first word is not used, usually the first or second key word or noun is used. Often, several different words or subjects must be checked before locating the information.

4. Notice the use of headings and subheadings. Rather than repeat the first word countless times, the subheading begins with the second key word or noun.

5. The *index* contains the page and line number for easy location once you have found the key word or noun.

6. On what page does the index begin? _____.

    On what page does the index end? _____.

    How many pages does the index contain? _____.

7. What is the first entry given in the index?

    _____

8. What is the last entry given in the index?

    _____

When you feel you have mastered this information, turn in this sheet and the copy of *Bartlett's* to be checked. When you have successfully completed this page, go on to sheet 10–4.

Name _____

Date _____

BARTLETT'S FAMILIAR QUOTATIONS: PRACTICE USING BARTLETT'S

DIRECTIONS: Locate a copy of *Bartlett's*. Bring it to your seat. Complete the following activities.

1. Suppose you remember part of a poem:

   > "In winter I get up at night
   > And dress by yellow candlelight."

   You do not remember the author, the title of the collection, or the rest of the poem. *Bartlett's* can help you.

   Turn to the index. If you look under "In" there is no entry. You remember that often the first word is not used, instead the first or second key word or noun is used.

   You look under the first key word or noun which is *winter*. Using the subheadings under winter, you locate:

   > in w. get up at night. A page number and line number are given.

   You remember that the lines are often shortened or abbreviated and that enough is given to tell you this is the line you want.

   Turn to the page given. Locate the line number. You have the information you need.

   The author is Robert Louis Stevenson.
   The title of the collection is *A Child's Garden of Verses*.
   The title of the poem is "Bed in Summer."

   The first stanza of the poem is:

   In winter I get up at night
   And dress by yellow candlelight.
   In summer quite the other way,
   I have to go to bed by day.

   If you need more stanzas or verses, locate the book in the poetry section.

Continue on to sheet 10–5 for more practice.

Name _____

Date _____

BARTLETT'S FAMILIAR QUOTATIONS :
PRACTICE USING *BARTLETT'S* **CONTINUED**

DIRECTIONS: Using *Bartlett's,* complete the following activities.

2. There is a famous quotation:

    "Give me liberty or give me death."

You do not know who said it, when it was said or why it was said, but you must find out for a homework assignment. *BARTLETT'S* can help you.

Turn to the index. Start with the word *give.* There are many subheadings under the word *give.* You go down the subheadings and locate:

    me liberty or death. A page number and line number follow.

You remember that the lines are often shortened or abbreviated and that enough is given to tell you that this is the line you want.

Turn to the page given. Locate the line number. You have the information you need.

    "give me liberty or give me death" is the final phrase of a speech.

By following the lb. back, you find that the phrase comes from a Speech in Virginia Convention, Richmond, Virginia, March 23, 1775. The author was Patrick Henry.

3. You need to find out who wrote the poem beginning:

    "I think that I shall never see
    a poem as lovely as a tree."

Turn to the index. There is no listing under I, think, that, shall, never, or see. The first key word or noun is *poem.* You go down the subheadings and locate:

    lovely as a tree. A page number and line are given.

Turn to the page given. Locate the line number. You have the information. The title of the poem is *Trees.* It was written by Joyce Kilmer.

When you feel you have mastered this information, go on to sheet 10–6.

Name _____

Date _____

BARTLETT'S FAMILIAR QUOTATIONS: REVIEW PAGE

DIRECTIONS: Cover the answers with your marker. Answer the following questions. Uncover the answers and check your work. Correct if necessary.

1. *Bartlett's* is a _____ book.   reference

2. *Bartlett's* is a collection of _____   famous

   _____.   sayings

3. *Bartlett's* contains more than 22,000 _____.   quotations

4. *Bartlett's* is arranged by authors from the _____   earliest

   authors to the _____.   latest

5. The *Index of Authors* is arranged _____.   alphabetically
                                                                              in the same
6. Ib. means _____.   place

7. Each author's works are arranged from the _____   earliest

   to _____ works.   latest

8. If you cannot locate the information through use of the first

   word, you use the _____ key word   second

   or _____.   noun

9. The subheadings begin with the _____   second

   key word or noun rather than repeating the main word.

10. *Bartlett's* was originated by _____   John Bartlett

    in _____.   1855

When you feel you have mastered this information, go on to sheet 10–7.

Name _____

Date _____

BARTLETT'S FAMILIAR QUOTATIONS: TEST FRAME

DIRECTIONS: Answer the following questions. As this is a test frame, no answers are given.

1. *Bartlett's* is a _____ book.

2. *Bartlett's* is a book of _____.

3. *Bartlett's* was first originated by _____

   in 1855.

4. *Bartlett's* contains more than 22,000 _____.

5. *Bartlett's* is arranged by authors from the _____ authors

   to the _____ authors.

6. The *Index of Authors* is arranged _____.

7. The *Index* of first lines in the back of the book is arranged

   _____.

8. The first word of the phrase, line, or sentence is not always used in the index. If the

   first word is not used, check the first or second _____

   or _____.

9. *Bartlett's* is generally used to locate the _____,

   the _____, or the _____

   when only a few words of the first line are known.

Turn in this sheet to be graded. When you pass the test, go on to sheet 10–8.

Name _____

Date _____

Activity 10–8

BARTLETT'S FAMILIAR QUOTATIONS: PRACTICE ACTIVITIES

DIRECTIONS: Using *Bartlett's,* complete the following activities.

1. Who stated, "Injustice anywhere is a threat to justice everywhere."

   Person _____

   Source _____

   _____

2. Who stated, "That's one small step for a man, one giant leap for mankind."

   Person _____

   Source _____

   _____

3. Who wrote, "No one can make you feel inferior without your consent."

   Author _____

   Source _____

   _____

4. Who wrote, "When one is a stranger to oneself then one is estranged from others too."

   Author _____

   Source _____

   _____

Turn in this sheet to be checked. When you have successfully completed this sheet you have completed the *Bartlett's Familiar Quotations* Unit.

UNIT 11

Roget's International Thesaurus

Name _____

Date _____

UNIT 11: *ROGET'S INTERNATIONAL THESAURUS*
CHECK-OFF SHEET

DIRECTIONS: Below you will find the names of each activity in UNIT 11. Check off each sheet as it is completed.

ROGET'S INTERNATIONAL THESAURUS —INTRODUCTION 11–1	
USING ROGET'S 11–2	
INDEX 11–3	
ACTIVITY PAGE 11–4	
REVIEW PAGE 11–5	
TEST FRAME 11–6	

Name _____

Date _____

ROGET'S INTERNATIONAL THESAURUS: INTRODUCTION

ROGET'S INTERNATIONAL THESAURUS is a reference book.

A thesaurus is a book of synonyms and related words.

Peter Mark Roget (1779 - 1869) prepared the first book of words organized by their meanings. The first edition was printed in 1852, and was titled, *Thesaurus of English Words and Phrases Classified and Arranged so as to Facilitate the Expression of Ideas and Assist in Literary Composition.*

Today, four editions later, it is known simply as *ROGET'S.* It is known as the most comprehensive work on synonyms and related words.

DIRECTIONS: Cover the answers with your marker. Answer the following questions. Uncover the answers and check your work. Correct if necessary.

1. *Roget's International Thesaurus* is a _____   reference

   book.

2. A thesaurus is a book of _____   synonyms

   and _____.   related words

4. The first edition of *Roget's* was prepared by

   _____ and   Peter Mark Roget

   was printed in _____.   1852

5. *Roget's* is known as the most comprehensive work on

   _____.   synonyms

When you feel you have mastered this information, go on to sheet 11–2.

Name _____

Date _____

ROGET'S INTERNATIONAL THESAURUS: USING ROGET'S

ROGET'S contains more than 256,000 synonyms and related words.

Roget's is divided into eight main class categories. Each main class is divided into various subclasses.

Roget's has no page numbers. Each word entry is given a number. Guide numbers at the top of the pages are used to locate the information needed.

DIRECTIONS: Locate a copy of *Roget's* or use the copy assigned to you. Cover the answers with your marker. Answer the following questions. Uncover the answers and check your work. Correct if necessary.

1. Locate the contents page. Locate the section, SYNOPSIS

    OF CATEGORIES.

2. What subject is given to CLASS TWO? _____   SPACE

3. CLASS FIVE: SENSATION is divided into _____   six

    main subclasses.

4. Open the book to any page. Notice the guide numbers at the

    top of the page. The first guide number is _____.   the first

    The guide number after the dash is _____. What   the last

    do the guide numbers mean? _____   numbered words
                                                                      on the page

    _____

    _____

When you feel you have mastered this information, go on to sheet 11–3.

Name _____

Date _____

ROGET'S INTERNATIONAL THESAURUS: INDEX

In order to locate information in *Roget's,* you must use the index.

The index, in the back of the book, is arranged alphabetically. Guide words at the top of the pages help you locate the words quickly.

Each entry is printed in dark type. The synonyms and related words are indented and listed under the main entry. They are labeled n. for noun, v. for verb, adj. for adjective, and adv. for adverb.

Locate the entry you wish and select the synonym that suits your purpose. The number listed next to the word will lead you to the information you seek.

© 1990 by The Center for Applied Research in Education

DIRECTIONS: Locate a copy of *Roget's* or use the one assigned to you. Cover the answers with your marker. Answer the following questions. Uncover the answers and check your work. Correct if necessary.

1. Locate the index in the back of the book.

2. The index is listed _____.   alphabetically

3. The main entry words are printed in _____   dark

    type.

4. What are the meanings of these abbreviations?

    n. _____   adj. _____   noun
                                                          adjective
    v. _____   adv. _____   verb
                                                          adverb

---

When you feel you have mastered this information, go on to sheet 11–4.

Name _____

Date _____

ROGET'S INTERNATIONAL THESAURUS: ACTIVITY PAGE

LIBRARY...
- Bookroom
- Collection
- Archive

Roget's Thesaurus

DIRECTIONS: Locate a copy of *Roget's* or use the one assigned to you. Cover the answers with your marker. Complete the following activities. Uncover the answers and check your work. Correct if necessary.

1. Locate the index.

2. Locate the word *bottle*. How many nouns are given? _____.   1

    How many verbs are given? _____.   4

3. Locate the noun *types of*. How many synonyms are given for

    the noun *bottle*? _____   16

    If you were looking for a synonym that meant a bottle used

    to carry water on a hiking trip, which entry would be the best?

    _____   canteen

4. Locate the word *research*. What noun is given?

    _____ What verbs are   investigation

                                                        experiment,

    given? _____   search

    Locate the subentry *search*. What subject is given the main

    number of 485? _____.   INQUIRY

    If you wanted a slang word for search, which synonym would

    you choose? _____   frisk

5. How many entries are listed under *INQUIRY*? _____   38

When you feel you have mastered this information, go on to sheet 11–5.

Name _____

Date _____

ROGET'S INTERNATIONAL THESAURUS: REVIEW PAGE

LIBRARY...
- Bookroom
- Collection
- Archive

DIRECTIONS: Cover the answers with your marker. Answer the following questions. Uncover the answers and check your work. Correct if necessary.

1. *Roget's International Thesaurus* is a

   _____ book.   reference

2. A thesaurus is a book of _____   synonyms

   and _____ words.   related

3. *Roget's* has no page numbers. To locate information in *Roget's*,

   you must use the _____ number.   word

4. The guide _____ at the top   numbers

   of each page give the _____ and _____   first

   number on each page.   last

5. The index is located in the _____   back

   of the book.

6. The index is arranged _____.   alphabetically

7. The index has _____ at the   guide words

   top of the pages to help locate the word.

8. Each word entry is printed in _____ type.   dark

9. The synonyms are listed under: nouns

   n. _____   adj. _____   adjectives

   verbs

   v. _____   adv. _____   adverbs

When you feel you have mastered this information, go on to sheet 11–6.

Name _____

Date _____

LIBRARY...
- Bookroom
- Collection
- Archive

ROGET'S INTERNATIONAL THESAURUS:
TEST FRAME

DIRECTIONS: Locate a copy of *Roget's* or use the one assigned to you. Answer the following questions.

1. *Roget's* is a reference book of _____.

2. To use *Roget's,* you look up a word in the _____.

3. As *Roget's* has no page numbers, to locate the information you must use a

   _____ system.

4. Look up the word *joy* in the index. What nouns are given?

   _____

   What verbs are given? _____

   Which synonym would you use for *joy* in beating an enemy opponent?

   _____

5. Look up the word *middle.* Which of the synonyms would you use for *middle* of a

   square? _____

6. Look up the word *walk.* Which entry would you turn to if you wanted a synonym

   for walking slowly? _____ Number _____

   Locate that synonym. What is the main subject shown in capital letters?

   _____

   If you wanted a word for a person advancing slowly using hands and feet, which two

   synonyms would probably be best? _____ _____

Hand in this sheet to be checked. When you have successfully completed this sheet, you have completed the Unit on *Roget's International Thesaurus.*

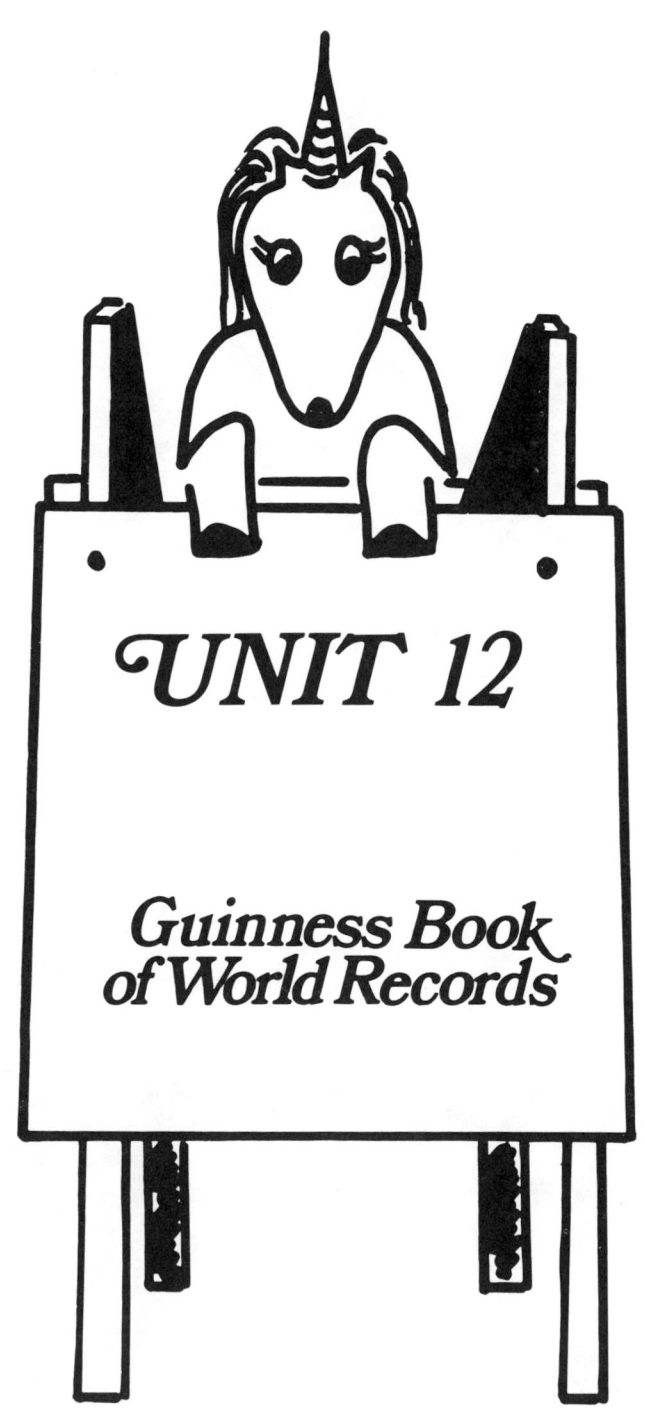

UNIT 12

Guinness Book
of World Records

Name _____

Date _____

UNIT 12: *GUINNESS BOOK OF WORLD RECORDS* CHECK-OFF SHEET

DIRECTIONS: Below you will find the names of each activity in UNIT 12. Check off each
sheet as it is completed.

GUINNESS BOOK OF WORLD RECORDS —INTRODUCTION 12–1	
RECORDS 12–2	
ACTIVITY PAGE 12–3	
REVIEW PAGE 12–4	
TEST FRAME 12–5	
USING GUINNESS 12–6	
ACTIVITY PAGE 12–7	
TEST FRAME 12–8	

Name _____

Date _____

GUINNESS BOOK OF WORLD RECORDS: INTRODUCTION

The *GUINNESS BOOK OF WORLD RECORDS* is a reference book of records which are carefully verified and documented. The publishers have the sole choice of which records will be included or excluded.

The *Guinness Book of World Records* was first published in England on August 27, 1955. By 1987, more than 57 million copies had been sold.

The *Guinness Book of World Records* can be used to check a record fact or for fascinating browsing through a variety of records and illustrations.

DIRECTIONS: Cover the answers with your marker. Answer the following questions. Uncover the answers and check your work. Correct if necessary.

1. The *Guinness Book of World Records* is a reference book of

    _____.   records

2. All records included in the *Guinness Book of World Records*

    are _____ and _____.   verified
                                                      documented

3. The _____ decide what records will   publishers

    be included or excluded.

4. The *Guinness Book of World Records* was first published in

    _____ on _____.   England
                                                      Aug. 27, 1955

5. By 1987, more than _____   57 million

    copies of *Guinness* had been sold.

When you feel you have mastered this information, go on to sheet 12–2.

Name _____

Date _____

12–2

GUINNESS BOOK OF WORLD RECORDS: RECORDS

All records published in the *Guinness Book of World Records* must meet certain rules. Most people try to break an already published record. Proof must be made by the participants.

1. The event must be covered by a television or radio station or a local or national newspaper.

2. Newspaper clippings and/or photographs must be included and signed by the reporter along with the name, place of publication, and date of publication of the newspaper.

3. Signatures of witnesses must be submitted.

4. For records that are times, log books that are complete, legible, and signed by the participants must be submitted.

Because the *Guinness Book of World Records* is so complete, it is unusual to have a new type of record published.

DIRECTIONS: Cover the answers with your marker. Answer the following questions. Uncover the answers and check your work. Correct if necessary.

1. All records published in the *Guinness Book of World Records*

    must meet _____.   certain rules

2. The proof of setting or breaking the record must be furnished

    by the _____.   participants

When you feel you have mastered this information, go on to sheet 12–3.

© 1990 by The Center for Applied Research in Education

Name _____

Date _____

GUINNESS BOOK OF WORLD RECORDS: ACTIVITY PAGE

The *Guinness Book of World Records* is divided into 15 sections.

The first section, *Is It a Record?,* discusses what records are published and how to submit record applications.

The main contents of the book are divided into 12 categories.

1. The Human Being	7. The World's Structures
2. The Living World	8. The Mechanical World
3. The Natural World	9. The Business World
4. The Universe and Space	10. The Human World
5. The Scientific World	11. Human Achievements
6. The Arts & Entertainment	12. The Sports World

All records must fall within these 12 categories.

The last two sections are:

Newly Verified Record
Index

© 1990 by The Center for Applied Research in Education

DIRECTIONS: Locate a copy of *Guinness Book of World Records* or use the one assigned to you. Complete the following activities.

1.   Locate the contents page. Read the section *Is It a Record?*.

2.   Check Chapters 1 - 12 to familiarize yourself with the categories. The categories should match up with the ones listed above.

3.   Locate the section *Newly Verified Records*. Notice that these records were received and verified, but were too late to be included in the main body of the book. Remember to check this section when checking a record to be sure you receive the correct information.

4.   Locate the index. When you need a fact quickly, the index is the best place to start.

When you feel you have mastered this information, go on to sheet 12–4.

Name _____

Date _____

GUINNESS BOOK OF WORLD RECORDS: REVIEW PAGE

DIRECTIONS: Cover the answers with your marker. Answer the following questions. Uncover the answers and check your work. Correct if necessary.

1. The *Guinness Book of World Records* is a reference book of

   _____.   records

2. All records included in the *Guinness Book of World Records*

   must be _____   verified

   and _____.   documented

3. The *Guinness Book of World Records* was first published in

   _____ in 1955.   England

4. The proof of setting or breaking a record must be furnished

   by the _____.   participants

5. The *Guinness Book of World Records* is divided into 12 main

   categories, plus three sections which are: _____   Is It a
                                                                Record?
   _____   Newly Verified
                                                                Records
   _____   Index

6. What proof must be submitted in order for a record to be

   published? _____   TV, radio or
                                                               newspaper coverage
   _____   signatures of
                                                               reporters and
   _____   witnesses, log books
                                                               photographs,
   _____   date of event

When you feel you have mastered this information, go on to sheet 12–5.

Name _____

Date _____

GUINNESS BOOK OF WORLD RECORDS:
TEST FRAME

© 1990 by The Center for Applied Research in Education

DIRECTIONS: Answer the following questions. As this is a test frame, no answers are given.

1. The *Guinness Book of World Records* is a reference book of _____.

2. Every record included in the *Guinness Book of World Records* has been thoroughly

    _____.

3. The *Guinness Book of World Records* was first published in _____.

4. The proof of setting a record or breaking a record must be furnished by the

    _____.

5. The *Guinness Book of World Records* is divided into 12 main categories, plus three

    sections. The three sections are:

    a. _____

    b. _____

    c. _____

6. What proof must be submitted in order for a record to be accepted?

    _____

    _____

    _____

    _____

Hand in this sheet to be checked. When you have successfully completed this sheet, go on to sheet 12–6.

Name _____

Date _____

GUINNESS BOOK OF WORLD RECORDS: USING GUINNESS

There are two ways to use the *Guinness Book of World Records:*

1. As a book of trivia, browsing and reading whatever catches your interest.

2. As a reference tool, to check a specific fact.

To locate specific information, it is wise to use the index.

DIRECTIONS: Locate a copy of *Guinness Book of World Records* or use the one assigned to you. Cover the answers with your marker. Answer the following questions. Uncover the answers and check your work. Correct if necessary.

1. Locate the index. How is the index arranged?

   _____.   alphabetically

2. Are the topics printed in dark type? _____   yes

3. Are the subtopics printed in dark type? _____   no

4. There are two types of page numbers.

   For example: Using a dash between 33 - 36

   Using a comma between 33, 36

   What is the meaning of the dash and the comma?

   Dash _____

   Comma _____

   information on the pages between; no information on the pages between

5. Which reference will give you more information?

   _____   the dash or 33 - 36

When you feel you have mastered this information, go on to sheet 12–7.

Name _____

Date _____

GUINNESS BOOK OF WORLD RECORDS: ACTIVITY PAGE

© 1990 by The Center for Applied Research in Education

DIRECTIONS: Locate a copy of *Guinness Book of World Records* or use the one assigned to you. Cover the answers with your marker. Answer the following questions. Uncover the answers and check your work. Correct if necessary.

1. Using the index, look up *aquamarine*.

   A _____ carat aquamarine was found near   520,000

   _____ Brazil in the year   Marambaia

   _____.   1910

2. Using the index, look up *education*.

   What university had the greatest enrollment (number of

   students) in the year 1984–1985?

   _____   State University
                                                                        of New York

   Number of students _____   156,175

3. Using the index, look up *swimming*.

   Who holds the duration record for treading water in the sea

   at Gzira, Malta?

   Name _____   Albert Rizzo
                                                                        108 hrs, 9 mins
   Time _____ Date _____   Sept 7–12, 1983

4. Using Newly Verified Records, what is the fastest road car?

   _____   Porsche 959

   Road-tested at a speed of _____   197 mph

When you feel you have mastered this information, go on to sheet 12–8.

GUINNESS BOOK OF WORLD RECORDS: TEST FRAME

DIRECTIONS: Locate a copy of *Guinness Book of World Records* or use the one assigned to you. Complete the following activities. As this is a test frame, no answers are given.

1. Who holds the record for the longest attack of hiccoughs?

   Name _____ of _____.

   He has hiccoughed about _____ times. The hiccoughs started

   when he was _____.

2. The record for the largest American or North Atlantic lobster is:

   Length _____. Weight _____.

   It was caught off _____ on _____.

3. The most expensive fabric is _____ cloth. It is

   made by _____ and costs _____ per meter.

4. What candy holds the record for the most sold? _____.

5. Who holds the record for the greatest number of pogo stick jumps?

   Name _____. Number _____.

   Where _____. When _____.

6. Where and when was the first football game televised?

   Where _____. When _____.

   Who played _____. Who won _____.

7. Who was the first gymnast to be awarded a perfect "10" or perfect score?

   _____.

Turn in this sheet to be checked. When you have successfully completed this sheet, you have completed the *Guinness Book of World Records* Unit.

UNIT 1—PARTS OF A BOOK

PARTS OF A BOOK: TEST FRAME

1. Spine
2. Cover
3. Text
4. Illustrations
5. Dust Jacket
6. Author
7. Title
8. Illustrator
9. Publisher
10. Place of Publication
11. Copyright
12. Copyright Date

TITLE PAGE: TEST FRAME

1. Title Page
2. a. Title
   b. Author
   c. Illustrator
   d. Publisher
   e. Place of Publication
3. Copyright Date
4. Title—The name of the book
   Author—The person who wrote the book
   Illustrator—The person who supplied the pictures
   Publisher—The company that produced the book
   Place of Publication—Where the publisher is located
5. The date the book is published

TABLE OF CONTENTS, PREFACE, FOREWORD, OR INTRODUCTION AND DEDICATION PAGE: TEST FRAME

1. Chapters
2. Contents, table of contents
3. Front
4. Titles
5. Preface, foreword, or introduction
6. Author, publisher, author
7. Front
8. Dedication
9. Front

TABLE OF CONTENTS, DEDICATION PAGE, PREFACE, FOREWORD, OR INTRODUCTION, APPENDIX, GLOSSARY, AND INDEX: TEST FRAME

1. Appendix
2. Glossary
3. Preface, foreword, or introduction
4. Dedication page
5. Table of contents
6. Index
7. Preface, foreword, or introduction dedication page, table of contents
8. Appendix, glossary, index

UNIT 2—CONCEPTS OF THE STORY

PARTS OF THE STORY: TEST FRAME

1. Setting
2. Character
3. Main character
4. Supporting characters
5. Plot
6. Quotation marks
7. Description
8. Dialogue
9. Beginning, middle, end

CONCEPTS OF THE STORY: TEST FRAME

1. Theme
2. Action
3. Genre
4. Style
5. Genre
6. Theme
7. Style
8. Action
9. Genre
10. Theme
11. Action

UNIT 3—CARD CATALOG

ALPHABETIZING

1. STU
2. NOP
3. VWX
4. KLM
5. XYZ
6. IJK
7. AB
8. UVW
9. MNO
10. PQR
11. EFG
12. LMN
13. JKL
14. CDE
15. GHI
16. ABC
17. RST
18. DEF
19. WXY
20. OPQ
21. BCD
22. TUV
23. QRS
24. HIJ
25. FGH
26. YZ

ALPHABETIZING AUTHORS, TITLES, AND SUBJECTS: TEST FRAME

1. Adler, C.S.
2. *The Biggest Bear*
3. *Crow Boy*
4. DINOSAURS
5. *Freckle Juice*
6. KANGAROOS
7. Lawson, Robert
8. *Many Moons*
9. NATURAL HISTORY
10. POETRY
11. Rey, H.A.
12. SPORTS
13. TREES
14. *The Wednesday Witch*
15. Yolen, Jane

OUTSIDE GUIDES: TEST FRAME

1. Kr - Lis 17
2. Wi - XYZ 30
3. Pr - Rh 23
4. Ir - Ko 16
5. Car - Ch 5
6. Fr - Ge 11
7. Cr - Dok 7
8. Pr - Rh 23
9. Fi - Fo 10
10. Stor - Th 27
11. Per - Po 22
12. Ci - Co 6
13. Mos - Ne 20
14. Cr - Dok 7
15. Ska - Sto 26

CATALOG CARDS: TEST FRAME

Author card
Subject card
Title card

Title card
Author card
Subject card

DECODING A CATALOG CARD: TEST FRAME

Call Number: DEC
Author: DeClements, Berthe
Title: *6th Grade Can Really Kill You*
Publisher: Viking Kestrel
Copyright Date: 1985

Kind of card: Author

Number of pages: 146

Call Number: DAH
Author: Dahl, Roald
Title: *Charlie and the Chocolate Factory*
Illustrator: Joseph Schindelman
Publisher: Knopf
Copyright Date: 1964

Kind of card: Title

Number of pages: 161

Call Number: BYA
Author: Byars, Betsy
Title: *The Animal, the Vegetable, and John D. Jones*
Illustrator: Ruth Sanderson
Publisher: Delacorte
Copyright Date: 1982

Kind of card: Subject

Number of Pages: 150

Call Number: 153.4N
Author: Nozaki Akihiro
Title: *Anno's Hat Tricks*
Illustrator: Mitsuma Anno
Publisher: Philomal Books
Copyright Date: 1985

Kind of card: Author

Number of pages: 41

LOCATING BOOKS ON THE SHELF: TEST FRAME

1. Alphabetically
2. Last
3. Alphabetically
4. Last
5. Number   last
6. Author
7. E   Author
8. Number   Author
9. Answers may vary
10. Not true
11. True
12. Not true
13. True

UNIT 4—ENCYCLOPEDIA

INTRODUCTION, ALPHABETICAL ARRANGEMENT, IMPORTANT RULES: TEST FRAME

1. Reference
2. Look up
3. People, places, things
4. Volume
5. Alphabetical
6. Last
7. Comma
8. First
9. Last
10. First
11. First
12. Spell
13. Unit   split

KEY WORDS: TEST FRAME

1. Entry
2. Article
3. Key word
4. Information
5. Key word
6. Dark
7. Canada; Washington, George
8. Alphabetical
9. Volume
10. Last

GUIDE WORDS: TEST FRAME

1. Top
2. Guide words
3. Left, right
4. First
5. Last
6. Guide
7. Back
8. Forward
9. Alphabetically, alphabetically

CROSS-REFERENCES AND HEADINGS: TEST FRAME

1. See   See also
2. See
3. See also
4. Divide
5. Main   sub
6. Dark
7. Main
8. Sub

PLAGIARISM AND PARAPHRASING: TEST FRAME

1. Copy
2. Plagiarism
3. Paraphrase
4. Facts
5. Meaning
6. Alphabetically
7. Final or last
8. Volume   page
9. Miss

UNIT 5—THE DEWEY DECIMAL CLASSIFICATION SYSTEM

TEST #1

1. Melvil Dewey
2. Nonfiction
3. Ten
4. Ten
5. Subject
6. Letter
7. Call number
8. Catalog card
   Book's spine
   Book pocket
   Book card

TEST #2

1. 700
2. 500
3. 400
4. 200
5. 000
6. 100
7. 800
8. 600
9. 900
10. 500
11. 700
12. 400
13. 700
14. 900
15. 500
16. 000
17. 700

UNIT 6—ALMANAC

INTRODUCTION: TEST FRAME

1. People, places, things
2. Yearly or annually
3. Current
4. *World Almanac and Book of Facts*
5. *The World Almanac*
6. Yearly or annually
7. November
8. Million
9. Front
10. Alphabetical

PRACTICE USING *The World Almanac*

1. Williamsburg, Virginia   1716
2. Maine
3. California   78
4. To bypass or overcome the 326 drop of Niagara Falls and the rapids of the Niagara River
5. Celebration of the Landing on Plymouth Rock, December 21
6. 10/22/1913   Dawson, New Mexico   263
7. Pyramids of Egypt
8. Titusville, Pennsylvania,   8/27/1859
9. Answers will vary

UNIT 7—ATLAS

INTRODUCTION: TEST FRAME

1. Maps, charts, pictures
2. Geographical atlas   Historical atlas
3. Physical maps, economic maps, and political maps
4. Political map
5. Physical map
6. Political map
7. Economic map
8. Political map
9. Physical map

HEMISPHERES, LONGITUDE, AND LATITUDE: TEST FRAME

1. Sphere
2. Hemisphere
3. Northern hemisphere
4. Southern hemisphere
5. Western hemisphere
6. Eastern hemisphere
7. Compass
8. Latitude
9. Equator   0
10. Longitude
11. Prime   0
12. Locate

GRID SQUARES AND SYMBOLS: TEST FRAME

1. Latitude   longitude
2. Intersecting
3. Letter
4. Letters   top   sides
5. Letters   one
6. Legend
7. Corner

8. Capital, scale of miles or kilometers, symbolic figures or picture language, altitude, roads, railroads, shipping lanes

FINAL TEST FRAME

1. Southern
2. Eastern
3. Hokkaido
4. Irish Sea
5. Bern
6. Egypt
7. Yukon
8. Pacific Ocean
9. Sicily

UNIT 8—THE *READERS' GUIDE*

INTRODUCTION: TEST FRAME

1. Magazine
2. Index
3. Subject, author
4. Media
5. Information
6. Subject of article
   Author of article
   Title of article
   Volume or issue number
   Page numbers of the article
   Date of the magazine
7. Monthly or bimonthly, quarterly, yearly

ABBREVIATIONS: ACTIVITY

1. biweekly
2. company
3. June
4. monthly
5. Squire
6. bibliography
7. Continued on later pages
8. March
9. Spring
10. Corporation
11. January
12. Department
13. supplement
14. May
15. part
16. year
17. Incorporated
18. Society
19. abridged
20. illustrated
21. bi-monthly
22. continued
23. Limited
24. Special
25. publisher, published, publishing
26. Summer
27. edited, edition, editor
28. translator, translated, translation
29. weekly
30. superintendent

DECODING: ACTIVITY SHEET

ROCK AND ROLL HALL OF FAME
Rock and Roll Hall of Fame dinner
J. Levenson
Illustrated
Down Beat
55
11
April 1988

No subject heading
hip, hip, but no hooray
Rooney, Andrew A.
illustrated
The Saturday Evening Post
260
14
April 1988

THE *READERS' GUIDE*: TEST FRAME

Subject heading; MOUNT EVEREST (CHINA AND NEPAL)
Title of article: The Adventures of National Geographical [expedition]
Author: No author given
il: article is illustrated
Volume number: 152
Page or pages: 12 - 15
Date of magazine: April 1988

Author: Steven S. Ross
Title: Software review for architects
Il: Article is illustrated
Volume number: 176
Page or pages: 125
+: Continued on later pages
Date of magazine: April 1988

UNIT 9—*FAMOUS FIRST FACTS*

TEST FRAME

1. Levi Hutchins, Concord, New Hampshire, 1787
2. *Encyclopedia Americana*, Francis Lieber, 13, 1833
3. Columbus, Ohio; July 4th
4. June 19; Pittsburgh, Pennsylvania

5. 1860, Washington D.C.
6. March 7, 1959; Capital Viscount; 1955
7. Charles Thurber; August 26, 1843
8. July 8th, 1916

UNIT 10—*BARTLETT'S FAMILIAR QUOTATIONS*

TEST FRAME

1. reference
2. famous sayings
3. John Bartlett
4. quotations
5. earliest, latest
6. alphabetically
7. alphabetically
8. key word, noun
9. author, title, whole work

PRACTICE ACTIVITIES

1. Martin Luther King
   Letter from the Birmingham jail
   In the *Atlantic Monthly,* August 1963

2. Neil Alden Armstrong
   On first stepping on the moon; July 20, 1969

3. Anna Eleanor Roosevelt
   This Is My Story

4. Anne Morrow Lindbergh
   Gift from the Sea; Chapter 3, 1955

UNIT 11—*ROGET'S INTERNATIONAL THESAURUS*

TEST FRAME

1. Synonyms
2. Index
3. Number
4. Happiness, merriment; be pleased, gloat, rejoice; gloat
5. Center
6. Slowness, SLOWNESS, creep, and crawl

UNIT 12—*GUINNESS BOOK OF WORLD RECORDS*

INTRODUCTION: TEST FRAME

1. Records
2. Verified
3. England
4. Participants
5. Is It a Record?
   Newly Verified Records
   Index

6. TV, radio, or newspaper coverage
   Signatures of reporters and witnesses
   Log books, photographs
   Date of event

FINAL TEST FRAME

1. Charles Osborne, Anthon, Iowa
   430 million
   Slaughtering a pig

2. 3 feet, 6 inches; 44 pounds, 6 ounces
   Nova Scotia, Canada; February 11, 1977

3. Vicuna
   Fuji Keori, Ltd.; Osaka, Japan
   $3,235 in 1983

4. Life Savers

5. Guy Stewart
   Number of jumps, 130,077
   Reading, Ohio
   March 8–9, 1985

6. Fordham University, 1939
   Fordham University and Waynesburg, Fordham 34 - 7

7. Nadia Comaneci, Olympics—1976

Pattern markers for Unit 1—Parts of the Book

Copy this page for the number of markers needed. Laminate, if possible.

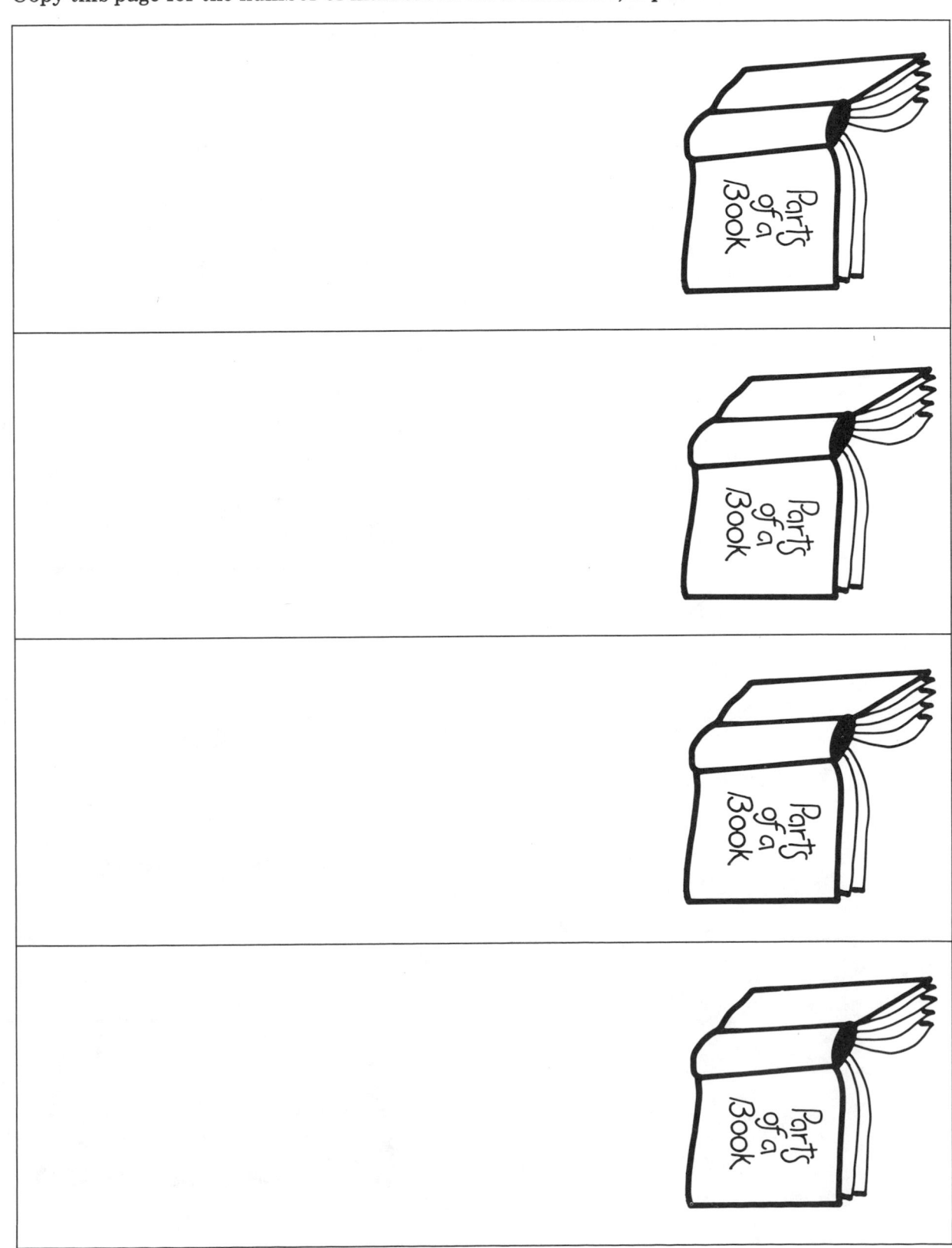

Pattern marker for Unit 2—Concepts of the Story.

Copy this page for the number of markers needed. Laminate, if possible.

Pattern marker for Unit 3—Card Catalog.

Copy this page for the number of markers needed. Laminate, if possible.

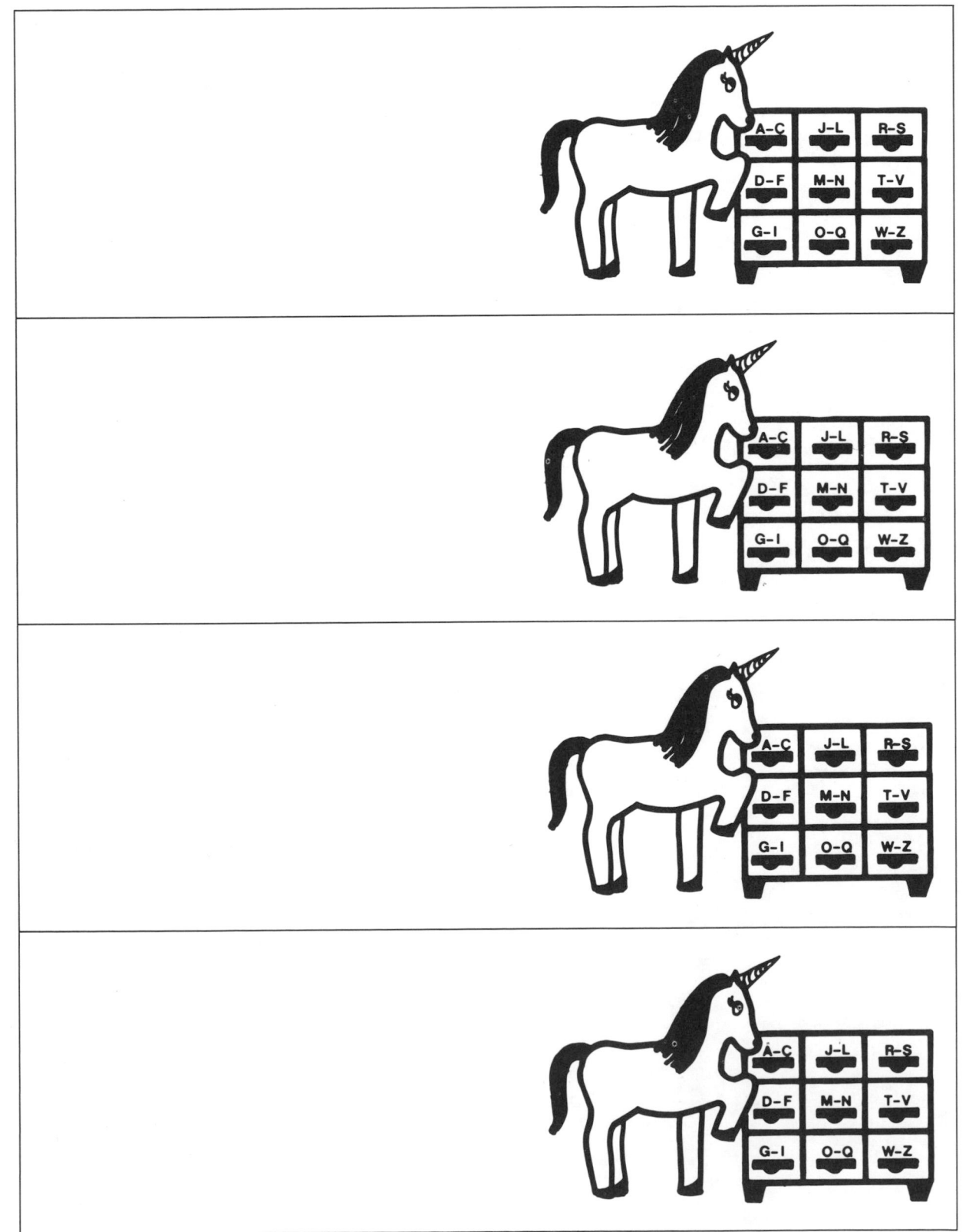

Pattern marker for Unit 4—Encyclopedia.

Copy this page for number of markers needed. Laminate, if possible.

Pattern marker for Unit 5—Dewey Decimal Classification System.

Copy this page for the number of markers needed. Laminate, if possible.

Pattern marker for Unit 6—Almanac.

Copy this page for the number of markers needed. Laminate, if necessary.

Pattern marker for Unit 7—Atlas.

Copy this page for the number of markers needed. Laminate, if possible.

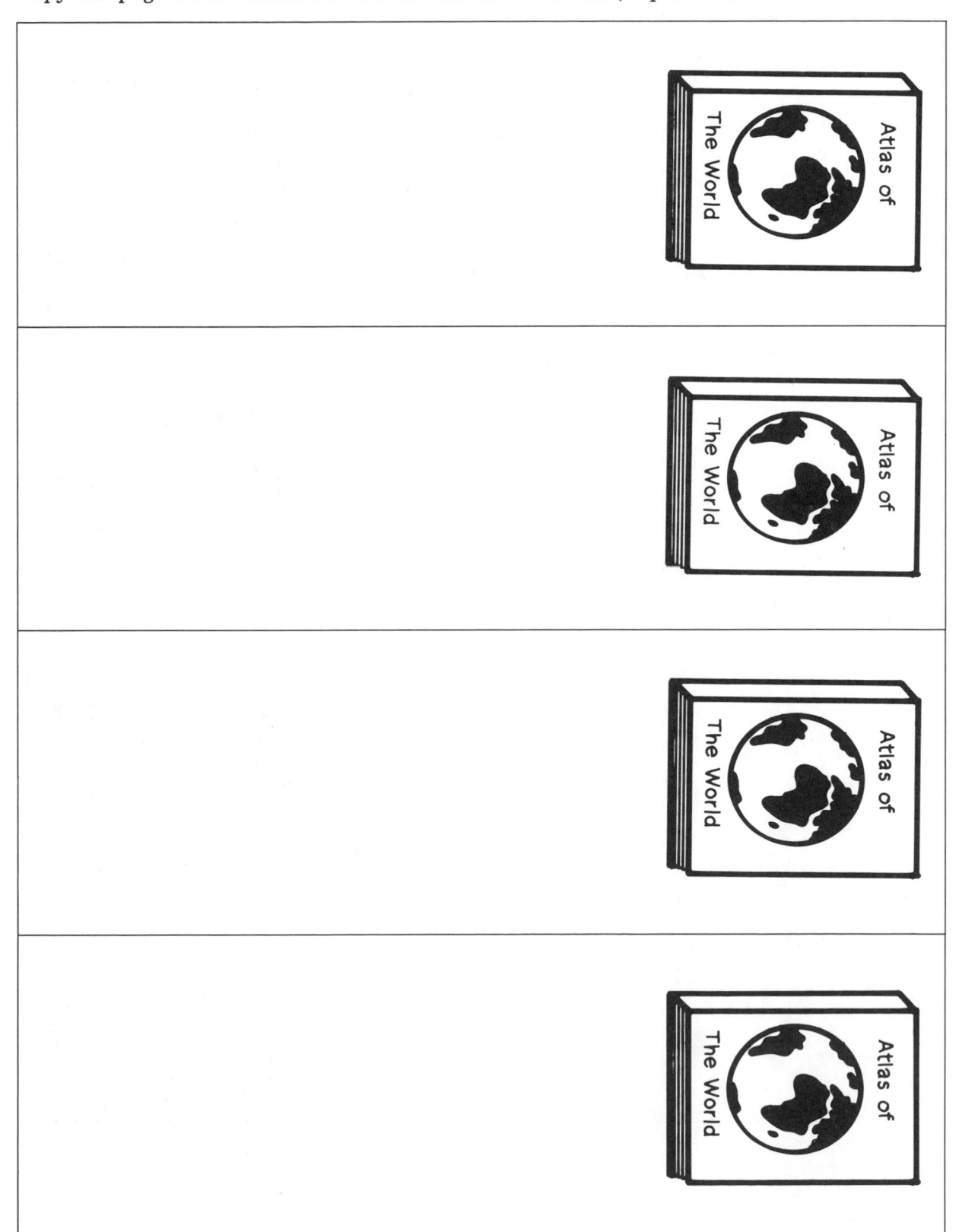

Pattern marker for Unit 8—*The Readers' Guide to Periodical Literature.*

Copy this page for the number of markers needed. Laminate, if possible.

Pattern marker for Unit 9—*Famous First Facts.*

Copy this page for the number of markers needed. Laminate, if possible.

Pattern marker for Unit 10—*Bartlett's Famous Quotations.*￼

Copy this page for the number of markers needed. Laminate, if possible.

Pattern marker for Unit 11—*Roget's International Thesaurus*.

Copy this page for the number of markers needed. Laminate, if possible.

Pattern marker for Unit 12—*Guinness Book of World Records*.

Copy this page for the number of markers needed. Laminate, if possible.